Judie Elmquist

The BIG Picture
Book of Mt. Pleasant
Michigan

YESTERYEARS to 2010

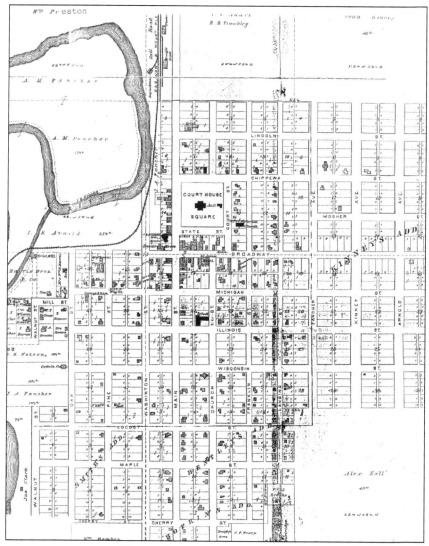

City of Mt. Pleasant 1889

The plat map above outlines the perimeters of Mt. Pleasant the year the community was established as a city. From 1875 until 1889 Mt. Pleasant was designated as a village.

ON THE COVER: On May 20, 2010, Fabiano Brothers, Inc. beverage distributors celebrated its 125th Anniversary by bringing the Budweiser Clydesdales to the Fabiano company's hometown, Mt. Pleasant, Michigan. Inset is the same corner in 1876, with a horse and wagon in front.

The BIG Picture Book of Mt. Pleasant Michigan

YESTERYEARS to 2010

Jack R. Westbrook

ORSB PUBLISHING

Mt. Pleasant, Michigan

ISBN: 10- 1453648895

1453648895

ISBN 13/EAN 13 9781453648896

Published by ORSB Publishing
POB 16 Mount Pleasant, Michigan, 48804-0016
989-773-5741

First Printing September, 2010
Second Printing October 27, 2010

This book is especially dedicated in memory of Dr. Mary Ellen Brandell, 1933-2010, whose love for and contributions to our community were boundless, enthusiastic and forever imprinted on the Mt. Pleasant cultural and historical landscape. She was a valuable contributor to this book, and to the lives of all who knew her. As was said in her eulogy September 29, 2010 "She called out the best in all of us."

Dedicated to anyone who ever wondered "What used to be there", and to those young and old with a passion for local history.

For longtime residents, the hope is you'll find your favorite places; to newcomers the hope is you will gain insight into the yesterdays of your adopted home; and, to future generations, the hope is you enjoy seeing how we looked at the beginning of the second decade of the
21st Century.

CONTENTS

Acknowledgements

In order to properly acknowledge everyone who had a hand in this book, we'd almost have to have a book as big as this one. Hundreds of people have called, talked on the street, in the market, in one case even in church, to tell us about their family, their business, or their relatives. This isn't my book, it's a book by people like James "Red" McLean, who knocked on the door one day to give me his entire file about the defunct Civitan's; like Janet Holman, who opened a whole new world with her pictures and story of her grandfather Civil War veteran John Neebes; like Jack Neyer, scouring his files to supply the names of his team in a 1989 picture; like Sandra Howard Wood searching a family album to find a photo I could remember seeing but couldn't find; like Jack Walton and Darcy Lapham talking about living in a tent in Nelson Park as children in the Great Depression and speaking with pride of their family's bravery and determination in surviving those days; and it's like a lot of people who I won't enumerate lest I sound like a newspeaker with "like" like" like". Those people who were able to furnish photos are acknowledged in the photo credit page at the end of the book. For those who furnished stories, leads and encouragement, accept my deepest thanks.

Thanks to my wife, Mary Lou, who supported me through this project.

Thanks to friend, genealogist, and co-author of another book Sherry Sponseller, whose research help was invaluable. A special hats off to Loren Anderson, whose sense of our local history and dedication top an eclectic collection of local memorabilia is astounding, and whose loan of photos to scan for this book is appreciated.

As always, thanks to Director Frank Boles, Achivist John Fierst, Susan Powers, Tanya Fox and Pat Thelan of Clarke Historical Library on the Mt. Pleasant campus of Central Michigan University for another fine job in helping locate photos, microfilms and files necessary to complete this job.

Most of all, thanks to the real experts on Mt. Pleasant history, retired Director of the Clarke Historical Library John Cumming and retired teacher Hudson Keenan, of Mt. Pleasant pioneer stock, who patiently suffer the esoteric and sometimes inconvenient questions of this amatuer.

The author with John Cumming and Hudson Keenan at a Clarke Historical Library reception.

Introduction

I thought I was done with local history book publishing at the end of 2009. Having written five local photographic histories since 2006, and consulted on the publication of three books by friends in the same period of time, I thought that was enough.

Then it started; early in 2010, comments in the *Morning Sun's* Sound Off feature about what used to be on Mission Street, some of them pretty inaccurate while thousands of images on my computer flashed on my screensaver, each silently saying "I should be in one of your books too", and the itch to do a more complete book on our area than *Mt. Pleasant: Then and Now*, the format of which was a bit restrictive.

A word about this books organization: the Downtown Chapter includes the original plat of the Mt. Pleasant settlement(encompassed by Washington, Franklin, Lincoln and Illinois Streets). Thereafter, if the address is South, it is in the South End chapter, if West, in the West Side chapter, etc. You get the idea.

Some of the photographs are less sharp than I would have preferred but the content of the picture was more important than the quality of the base print in my opinion, so some were included with all their faded, over exposed, underexposed, warts and wrinkles.

This work is not so much an all-inclusive history as it is a letter to my friends, today and in the distant future, about some Mt. Pleasant places, people, and local lore I know about in 2010. I know, and so will the reader, there are a lot of locations and events not included. But I Also know no single reader will already know everything in this book.

As always, no person or business has been intentionally omitted or emphasized. The main criterion for being included was making sure I had the picture to use. No effort of this size can be done without the occasional "ouch" of an inadvertent mistake. Let me know of them and they will be corrected in later printings.

When I started this project, I thought I would use every picture I have. Now I have almost again as many as I've used.

If you've ever fished a trout stream and kept fishing "one more hole" until you step out of the stream and realize you are miles from where you started without realizing how far you'd traveled, you can understand my dilemma. I've fished a lot of historical photo holes this past four years and now it's time to go home, even though there are still trout left in the stream.

It's time for me to read some books instead of writing them … with the hope you've enjoyed this family album of our town.

Thanks for your continued interest.

J.R.W. Mt. Pleasant, Michigan, September 6, 2010

CHAPTER 1: GENERAL HISTORY

A salute to the men who caused Mt. Pleasant to be built – Lumbermen plied the rivers of Michigan driving logs from forests depth to sawmill and market. The rivers were Michigan's first highways. Along the way, they needed riverside way-stations to replenish provisions, dine, drink, bathe, sleep in a bed and in general enjoy the creature comforts of a settled place. After David Ward timbered his 200 acres on the high banks of the Chippewa River, he platted a village and sold the platted land to the Morton Brothers, who built the Morton House as Mt. Pleasant's first hotel, to accommodate the river men. The county seat located here later from Indian Mills, commemorated by the plaque dedicated by the Daughters of the American Revolution in 1931, below. All the other stuff came later.

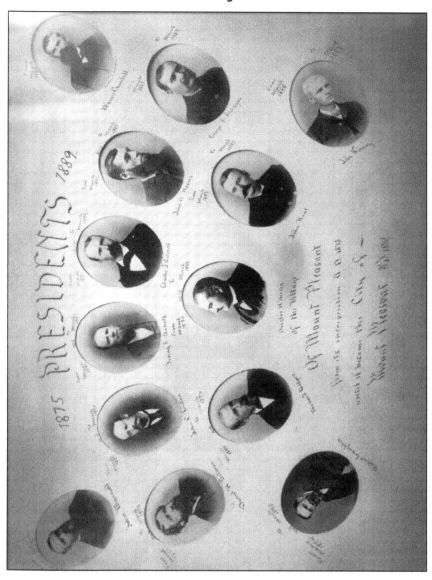

Mt. Pleasant Village Presidents 1875-1889 - Mt. Pleasant was incorporated as a village in 1875 and became the City of Mt. Pleasant in 1889. Serving as President of the community during those interim years were: John Marshall 1875-76; Daniel H. Gilman 1877-79; John T. Leaton 1879-80; Irving F. Arnold 1880-81; Charles T. Russell 1881-82; John H. Harris 1882-83; George T. Granger 1883-84; Robert Coughlin 1884-85; Thomas Fordyce 1885-86; Douglas Halson 1886-87; John Kane 1887-88; John Kinney 1888-89; and Warner Churchill 1889.

City of Mt. Pleasant Mayors 1889 - 2010

1889	Lewis E. Royal
1890-91	M.Deveraux
1892	E. D. Wheaton
1893	Cornelius Bennett
1894	Tobias Begey
1895	I. A. Fancher
1896-97	M. Deveraux
1898-99	C. M. Brooks
1900-01	Levi Shafer
1902	Arthur N. Ward
1903-05	H. Edward Deuel
1906	H. A. Miller
1907	M. Deveraux
1908	Walter Snider
1909-10	H. Edward Deuel
1911	Fred Russell
1912	H. Edward Deuel
1913	Fred Newberry
1914-15	H. Edward Deuel
1916-17	Walter W. Russell
1918	W. S. Horn
1919	L. A. Kauffman
	Luman Birch
1920	Fred Russell
1921-27	W. H. Pearce
1927-28	M. T. Kenney
1929-33	E. O. Harris
1934	R. T. Kane
1935-37	W. S. Horn
1938-39	John Benford
1940	Charles E. Smith
1941-44	F. E. Robinson
1945	N. D. Gover

1946	R. T. Kane
1947	J. D. Leonard
1948	T. M. McShea
1949	I. W. Hartman
1950-51	Norman X. Lyon
1952	Del Conkright
1953-54	E. Lee Johnson
1955	J. J. Rush
1956-57	G. R. Denison
1958-59	Douglas McFarlane, Sr.
1960	K. P. Wood
1961	R. F. Sweeney
1962-63	Jackson K. Beatty
1963	J. Dean Eckersley
1964	C. F. Dumon
	Norman Zuker
	J. Dean Eckersley
1966	J. Dean Eckersley
1967-68	Raymond O. Planteroth
1969	J. Hudson Keenan
1970	L. A. Johns
1971	Paul Hubscher
1972	Sam Wunderbaum
1973	Barton LaBelle
1974	J. Hudson Keenan
1975	Paul Hubscher
1976	J. E. Johnson
1977	W. Sidney Smith
	Sibyl M. Ellis
1978	Thaddeus Zolty
1979	Sibyl M. Ellis
1980	James Phillips
1981	Gary Knight
1982	Thomas Weirich

1983	Douglas D. McFarlane, Jr.
1984	Gary Knight
1985	Sibyl M. Ellis
1986	G. Patrick Doyle
1987	Donald J. Breckon
	Conrad A. English
1988	Conrad A. English
1989	William L. McCarthy
1990	Douglas D. McFarlane, Jr.
1991	Conrad A. English
1992	Susan Kay Smith
1993	Kenneth C. Bovee
1994	Robert S. Trullinger
1995	Donald N. Sowle
1996	Susan Kay Smith
1997	Gerald D. Cassel
1998	Sharon M. Tilmann
1999	Michael R. Pittsley
2000-01	Albert Kaufmann, Jr.
2002	Michael R. Pittsley
2003	Adam A. Miller
2004	Matthew R. Showalter
2005	Adam A. Miller
2006	Cynthia Bradley Kilmer
2007-08	Jon Joslin
2009-10	Jim Holton

CHAPTER 2: DOWNTOWN

The earliest Downtown photos we were able to find are these apparently taken from the top of the Isabella County courthouse about the time construction began in 1876. The view in the picture, above, is looking south from the courthouse in the 200 block of North Main Street. The street running diagonally left to right in the left quadrant of the shot is Church Street, later Normal, then College, then University. The large white building is the St. James Hotel, which burned in 1878. Some evidences of the devastation of the August 5, 1875, fire are apparent in the vacant lots of the foreground and along East Broadway, we're looking at their backs. Those wooden buildings would ultimately be replaced by brick structures like those seen upper right.

Below, shifting the angle slightly to the southwest, we see the back of the Fancher building, left, at the northeast corner of Broadway and Main. Across the street to the right, offset from Main Street, diagonal left to right, bottom, is Mt. Pleasant's original hotel, the Morton House, destined to become the Bamber House, replaced by a brick structure when it became the Donovan House and eventually the Park Hotel.

Addresses are unknown for the photographs on this page, but we do have people identification.

Left is the offices of Enterprise Printers in 1888 with the staff posing in front of a wood frame building. Left to right are: A. Butterin, C. W. Chase, Ora May Sanford, A. S. Courtland, M. L. Sherman, and an unidentified passer-by, a bane to the existence of researchers. A pox upon whoever did not write down her name or location..

Right are business neighbors J. Freeman and Cox & Peake. Proudly posing in front of their establishments of unknown location are, left to right: a Mr. Sheldon, J. C. Freeman, Mr. Peake, and Mr. Cox. Again, a second pox on people who do not record dates on photographs. Not that it will be an issue in future years, when those who deal in digital images will be scrupulous about labeling the subjects.
Yeah.
Of Course.

CHAPTER 2:DOWNTOWN
NORTH MAIN - BROADWAY TO CHIPPEWA STREET

101-107 North Main Street in 1920 - The venerable Park Hotel at the northwest corner of Main and Broadway was built as the Morton House, became the Bamber House, bought by Patrick Donovan, right below, with son Michael. Donovan bought the wood frame hostelry around the turn of the 20th Century, tore it down and built the Donovan House on the site. Next door to the right, north, is the Campbell Building.

107 North Main Street - The Campbell Building was built in 1914 by C. W. Campbell , a successful Mt. Pleasant Hardware dealer. Shown above in the last years of its life, the building was home to Campbell Merchantile, Giant Super Market's first store, Coleman Peters Radio and Television, United Discount and Mt. Pleasant's first Yankee Store. Jack's Bar, earlier the Eat Well Restaurant, sits beside the Campbell Building to the north.

In October 1941, Giant Super Market opened the first store of what would grow to a nine-location chain of grocery mega-markets throughout the state. Partnering with Giantway discount department stores, the Giant-Giantway alliance forged the first of the one-roof super stores, well ahead of Kmart, Meijer, Target, and Wal-Mart.

107-109 North Main Street (continued) - The Park Hotel was gone, replaced by a vacant lot used in winter as the site of Santa's House, and the neighbor eatery to the north had already met the wrecking ball, above, when in the winter of 1973, the Campbell Building was turned to a pile of brick, below. Note in the upper right of the lower photo that Mosher Street had already been punched through from Franklin Street to curve around behind the site to Broadway at Washington.

101-109 North Main - Driver Will Casner pauses along his street sprinkling route in 1914, midway between the Donovan House, C. W. Campbell Merchantile and Eat Well Restaurant, to pose with the equipment bought by Howard Chatterton to keep the dust down in the downtown area.

117 North Main - Harley and Mabel Stacy, proprietors, left, pose in front of Stacy's Variety Store. The store operated only a short time in the late 1920s just into the 1930s, when Harley died. In 2010, both locations are occupied by the Town Center.

101-109 North Main – In the U. S. Bicentennial Year, 1975, the northwest corner of Main and Broadway became Freedom Square and in a fit of archtectural faddish, Mt. Pleasant's downtown became a maze of concrete posts and planters, named "tank traps" by a bemused public. By 1988, above, Riverview Apartments had been constructed by the city as first a senior citizens and now a low income housing complex.

100-200 blocks North Main west side – In 1947, below, the first two blocks of the west side of North Main Street, past the Campbell Building were: 111 - Eat Well Restaurant; 115 – Main Billard Room, American Laundry behind 115; 117 - McKillip Electric; 121 – Falsetta's Bar; 123 - used furniture store; 125 – Pyretts Shoe Repair; 127 – Central Printers; 201 – Catherines Beauty & Barber Shop; 205 – Hughes Tool; 209 – Merritt Oil Co. filling station; 211-213 A & P grocery store; 225 Floyd T. Mitchell residence and 233 Northway Clinic and Hospital.

Court Street runs north from 200 East Broadway and is shown below in the late 1940s. For perspective, Mosher Street would eventually run diagonally from the left side of this photo. The building to the right is the Bennett Hotel. The numbers are all even since State Street, Jockey Alley, runs east to west from Court to Main Street. In 1947, those occupying Court Street were, above, right to left; 104 – Gulf Refining; 106 Nu-Way Cleaners; 108 - Brien Insurance; 110 - Landon Barber Shop; 112 – Vern Turner Ford Sales; and 116 – I.O.O.F., International Order of Odd Fellows, Hall.

In 1947, sun-struck photo above, Verne Turner bought the Ford dealership from Floyd Johnson, Harper Clifford bought the dealership from Turner and later sold it to the Krapohl Brothers, Bob and Harold. In the 1970s, Fish Head Aquariums, Little Red Shoe House and Mt. Pleasant Schwinn Bicycle populated the short street.

2010 business residents of Court Street are, below, right to left: 102 - The Blue Gator; 104 - Sha-Boom Lounge; 112 – Ross & Ross CPAs, Douglas McDonald CPA; and, 116 – Mt. Pleasant Abstract and Title.

202-204 Court Street - Built in 1936 as the new McArthur-Strange Hospital at 204 Court, above, was two stories high, adjacent to the Bronstetter Hospital at 202 Court. Known as the Wood Building, and

used for storage and labs for the Bronstetter Hospital. After 1932, the hospital name changed to the McArthur-Strange Hospital.

202 Court was razed to accommodate, left, the push-through of Mosher Street to Main in the 1970s.

In 2010, below, the Wood building is occupied in the southwest corner by Tom and Donna Murphy as a residence, with the rest of the building occupied by Always Me Bail Bonds; Cindy Karszewski CPA and Jostens.

207 Court Street - Sheriff Palmer Landon, above, stands in front of the Isabella County Sheriff's Department/Jail/Sheriff's residence, built in 1882 to replace a clapboard structure built in 1870 on the same site. The modern Isabella County Jail, below, replaced the Victorian-era building in 1962.

205-209 North Main – A group of 1950s schoolkids decorate the windows of Carl's Furniture Store at 205 North Main in a scene that also captures a rare photo of the Merritt Oil Company City's Service gasoline filling station and garage at 209 North Main.

The 205 North Main location was variously occupied by Elmore's Furniture Display and, upstairs, the Mt. Pleasant Elks Club. After Carl's Furniture and the Elks Club, the building was home to the offices of Lynch, Gallagher and Lynch attorneys, upstairs, and the Isabella County Building Annex. The two story structure was demolished in 2004 to make room for a planned bronze sculpture park that never materialized but now holds a free standing clock and benches at the northwest quadrant of the Mosher-Main turn-about.

At 209 North Main was one of several downtown gasoline filling stations, first the Stutting Oil Company and then the Merritt Oil Company stations. The author was delighted to find this photo since his grandfather, Walter Scott Westbrook, worked part time at the Merritt station in the early 1940s. The painted cement block structure was demolished to allow expanded parking for 215 North Main in the late 1950s.

215 North Main – This was the site of Janet "Jennie" McLeod Brodie's photograph studio from where she captured the first photo image of the wood frame original Isabella County Court House across the street in 1860. Built as Kluge Grocery, the building hosted the A & P Food Store from 1942, above, until its 1961 move to 709 East Broadway.

The building was purchased by Jack Neyer and Milton Marks for $25,000 while vacant in 1962, below, who remodeled and opened Marney's, a teen dance hall playing current music of the day and teens could dance for a fifty cent admission fee. Like most businessess that try to answer the eternal teen lament "there's nothing to do in this town", Marney's was soon just a memory by the mid-1960s.

215 North Main (continued) – In 1966, real estate broker Jerry Mc Farlane purchased the vacant Marney's/A & P building from Neyer and Marks and later that year sold it to PANAX Publishers, who moved the Daily Times-News into the building, changing the newspaper's name to the Morning Sun in 1977. The Mitchell home on the adjoining north lot, was razed to create the newspaper's north parking lot.

When the Morning Sun moved to 711 West Pickard Street in the summer of 2000, the building was not vacant long. Again the structure was remodeled and opened in August 2001 as home of the accounting firm Boge Wybenga & Bradley PC.

225 North Main was the elegant home of business and civic leader Floyd T. Mitchell, who moved to Mt. Pleasant from Weidman in 1924 with his wife Mable, who died in December, 1942. In October, 1947, Mitchell married Gaynelle Cleaner of Big Rapids and brought her to the Mt. Pleasant mansion. Floyd Mitchell died March 1, 1948, but Gaynelle lived on in the home in grand style. Gaynelle's thoroughbred horse was housed in a stable behind her home and her rides through nearby Island Park in riding togs complete with jodphurs, along with her live-in servants and chauffered rides through town were the stuff of local legend. She sold the house in 1969 to the neighboring property owners and returned to Big Rapids, where she died in October, 1976. The property is now the north parking lot for Boge Wybenga & Bradley PC.

304-328 North Main – The oldest surviving home in Mt. Pleasant, at the time of the 1963 celebration of the town's 1863 platting, was the house at the northeast corner of Chippewa and North Main, above. Built by Dr. E. Burt, the house was sold to William W. Preston when his family arrived here in 1863.

The three apartment houses, two wood frame and one brick, were built to meet the the 1930s Mt. Pleasant housing crunch prompted by the oil "boom" following the 1928 discovery of the Mt. Pleasant Field. All four 300 block north Main structures were demolished to make room for the expansion of the Isabella County Building complex.

233 North Main is the site of the first Mt. Pleasant home Isaac A. Fancher built in 1863. Isaac Fancher was born September 30, 1833, in Montgomery, New York. He was married June 6, 1860, to Althea Preston at Java, New York, shortly after he left law school. After a stint of prospecting for silver in Nevada, the Fanchers returned from the west to Kilbourn City, Wisconsin, where his parents had moved from New York state. Shortly thereafter, his wife received word that her father, Albert Preston, brother Wallace, sister Ellen and her husband Samuel Woodworth, had moved to a tiny settlement in central Michigan named Mt. Pleasant, where Ellen was the first schoolteacher in the newly named Isabella County seat. Probably at the behest of Althea, the young Fancher family moved to Mt. Pleasant.

Lumberman David Ward had timbered off his 200 acre holdings on the high ground beside the Chippewa River beginning in 1856. In 1860, he platted a village and named it Mt. Pleasant because the area reminded him of his boyhood home in Pleasant Valley, and the high banks of the Chippewa River where his land was located was reminiscent of a small mountain. In 1860 Ward gave the new Isabella County government five acres if they would

Isaac A. Fancher about 1900.

233 North Main (continued)

move the county seat to his village, which he then sold to George Morton, a New York investor, George's nephew Harvey Morton and wife Cordelia were sent to promote the new village.

When 30 year-old Isaac Fancher arrived in Mt. Pleasant on July 4, 1862, there were two houses.

A crude cabin served as the first County Building just south of Mr. Preston's home at the corner of Main and Chippewa streets. Harvey Morton, who was building a hotel at the corner of what is now Main and Broadway to house potential prospective buyers of lots in the new village, sold Isaac Fancher three lots along Main Street. Fancher suggested that a new survey be done since the original plat had not been registered. One of Fancher's first Mt. Pleasant jobs was conducting the first registered plat of the village.

The need for better roads, railroads, schools and businesses was apparent to him and he set about on what would be a 71 year upbuilding of Mt. Pleasant from a backwoods frontier people cluster to a city. He built a home catty-cornered from his father-in-law's house.

He played a key role in bringing a number of entities to town to enhance community growth, including: the railroads; Central Michigan Normal School (now Central Michigan University); and the United States Indian Schools to the city. He was interested in lumber mills and built the Fancher block, one of the town's first commercial buildings, at the southeast corner of Main and Broadway.

Fancher served terms in both the Michigan Senate and Michigan House of Representatives, as well as being Mayor of Mt. Pleasant, City Attorney, County Surveyor, and Michigan Road Commissioner.

Around 1900, he sold most of his business interests to focus on his legal career, distinguishing himself as one of Middle Michigan's leading attorneys. Fancher Avenue in Mt. Pleasant, one of the city's principal north-south thoroughfares, is

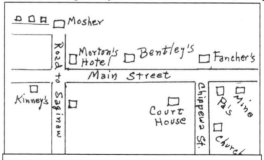

Ellen Woodworth's sketch of 1864 Mt. Pleasant, included in her letter to her husband Samuel when he was away in the Civil War.

named for Isaac A. Fancher, as is Fancher Elementary School at 801 South Kinney Street.

233 North Main (continued)

When Fancher died at 101 years old on March 19, 1934, the *Isabella County Times* said "Mr. Fancher continued to manifest a keen interest in this community and its welfare to the time of his death."

Fancher's greatest legacy to the area, however, is his massive exhaustively detailed history book PAST AND PRESENT OF ISABELLA COUNTY MICHIGAN, published in 1911 by B. F. Bowen & Company of Indianapolis, Indiana. The best history of the county ever published and a seminal work for local historians, this rare 737 page illustrated volume details the history of the county and it's people in mind-boggling detail … a valued resource for this and other local history authors.

Fifty properties in and around Mt. Pleasant had deeds registered in Isaac Fancher's name over the years and records are obscure as to how long he occupied the 233 North Main address or the succession of home residents there until relatively recent times.

Following Fancher's death in 1934, the property was purchased by osteopathic Dr. R. A. Northway, who had come to Mt. Pleasant in 1910 and established offices first in the Dusenbury Building, then in the Exchange Bank Building, both downtown, before moving his practice to 233 North Main. He suspended operations of his clinic there about 1954, when failing health sent him to a convalescent home in Gladwin.

The property was vacant until May of 1958, when it was purchased by Peter and Anne Reale, ironically also from New York state, who rehabilitated the aging structure, adding on and operating a beauty salon at that location for many years.

309 North Main was the home of Dr. Sheridan Ellsworth Gardiner, who graduated from the Medical College of Philadelphia in 1893 and practiced medicine in his native New York state before coming to Mt. Pleasant and establishing offices above Dittman's Shoe Store at 133 East Broadway in 1898. In 1944, the office was moved to his home. "They made me move to the house when they thought I was going to die" he is quoted as saying in a 1956 newspaper article when he was determined by the American Medical Association to be the oldest active medical practitioner in the United States.

Gardiner organized the first Isabella County Medical Society and was its secretary for many years. Later Clare and Gratiot counties were included and the organization became the G.I.C. Medical Society, of which Gardiner was president in 1918. He was elected delegate to the Michigan Medical Society. Dr. Gardiner was Mt. Pleasant City Health Officer for about forty years. He was also secretary of the United States Pension Board.

None of those laudable duties swayed him from treating patients. He made house calls throughout the county until he was 70 and house calls in the city until he was 80. After that he focused on the work of an oculist.

Gardiner's wife, the former Blanche Irish, died in 1954 and her niece, Dorothy Irish came to live with them in 1927 and remained as Gardiner's assistant. Blanche died in 1954 and in 1956, S. E. Gardiner married Dorothy. He died at home, at 94 years of age, November 23, 1959, having actively practiced medicine until just a few weeks before.

200 North Main Street – In 1860, voters of the year-old Isabella County voted to move the county seat about three miles southwest from Isabella City to the five acres in newly-platted Mt. Pleasant donated by David Ward on the condition the county seat be moved to the settlement.

The first county building was a wood frame structure at the north end of the acreage, which accounts for all of the 200 block of North Main Street, above. In 1876, construction began, below, in the middle of the tract of a Victorian-style courthouse which opened in 1877.

In 1972, the elegant courthouse building was replaced by the monotonously modern glass and aluminum structure below.

State Street/Jockey Alley – State Street, between Main and Court streets just south of the Isabella County courthouse, has been persistently known as "Jockey Alley". Those conducting county business "jockeyed" for a place to park horses and carriages, above. Later, automobiles replaced the carriages and the municipal parking lot continues to modern times to be known colloquially as Jockey Alley. In 1947, great hue and cry erupted from an anguished parking public when the Mt. Pleasant City Commission decided to install parking meters along the sacrosanct open parking area on the north side of "Jockey Alley". In 1948, the discovery was made that the meters were six to eighteen inches onto county land (the five acres set aside for the county complex in 1860) and the meters were removed, to be forevermore replaced by signs restricting parking time … peace returned to the land.

State Street/Jockey Alley (continued) – Once memories faded sufficiently, parking meters returned for a time to State Street in the mid-1950s, as shown in this view of the courthouse looking northeast, probably taken by Kathleen Peters from a window in the Campbell Building, tallest downtown structure at the time. The parking meters would finally be removed permanently when Mission Street commerce began to increase competition to downtown businesses. A "free parking downtown" slogan was trotted out as a potential customer inducement and another piece of governmental myopic flaw in previous master plans after being subjected to the 20-20 vision of hindsight.

Mosher Street was pushed through westward from Franklin Street, curving to join Washington at Broadway in 1874, perhaps in honor of General Mosher, who owned the property where Broadway ended at Washington Street in the original plat of Mt. Pleasant. General Mosher sold his lots to the village of Mt. Pleasant in 1878 and Broadway Street, originally called simply "the road to Saginaw" was built west to the Chippewa River.

CHAPTER 2:DOWNTOWN
SOUTH MAIN - BROADWAY TO ILLINOIS STREET

108 South Main, above in 1906, was the founding site of the Exchange Savings Bank, first established as a private enterprise in 1881 by G. A. Dusenbury & Company, operated until 1888, when it was succeeded by Dusenbury, Nelson & Company, which continued as a private institution, but adopted the name of Exchange Bank. In May, 1894, the Exchange Savings Bank was organized and incorporated under Michigan law. The Bank remained in this location until moving to the southeast corner of Main and Broadway in 1909.

The address was then occupied by P. Cory Taylor's Drug Store. Taylor had come to town in 1888 and had operated from a number of locations, including next door at 106 South Main, before renovating the Exchange Bank location when that firm moved. The 106 locale then became home to the Minto Woodruff insurance firm. Taylor's Drug Store would become the Mt. Pleasant Drug Store and later Smith's Drug Store. The Smith Brothers would later move the drugstore to the southeast corner of Michigan and Main Streets into the Carpenter Building, where Central Michigan University got its start as Central Michigan Business Institute and Normal School on the second floor in 1892.

108 South Main (continued) became the location of Dick Shook's Western Auto store in 1958. That's Dick in the doorway of his new business, between the original Blackstone Lounge to the south and Woodruff Insurance Agency to the north. In the 1980s, below, the business address was occupied by Linns Camera Shop.

108 South Main (continued) is far left, above, in 1988 when Main Street had been converted from a two way traffic venue to one-way headed north beyond Illionis Street to end at Pickard. By this time the corner location was occupied by Downtown Drug Store, with Norm Curtis' discount store next door in the former Woodruff Insurance/Frank Powell Realty/Bob Reynolds State Farm Insurance locale.

The Michigan Oil & Gas News magazine, still in operation in 2010, got its start upstairs in this building at 108 in 1933, but quickly was moved when the rumble of the printing press distressed business neighbors.

In 2010, below, the location is part of a three storefront occupancy of Firstbank.

112 South Main Street was the Blackstone Bar and Restaurant from the 1930s until the mid-1970s, owned and managed for most of those years by Pete Spiris and Sam Poulus, above. The Blackstone was the "in place" for Mt. Pleasant nightlife, with a dance hall upstairs and band music on the weekends. The Blackstone later sold to Tom McEvoy, who moved the business to 212 West Michigan. McEvoy sold to Emil Sacco in the 1990s, who in turn sold to the 2010 owners Steve and Don Bissell. Today, the address is occupied by Allied Hearing, below.

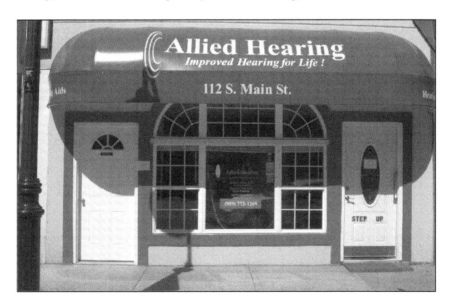

114 South Main Street in 1881, above, was where Frank A. Sweeney (doorway) opened a mercantile store. In the 1940s, it was Johnson Shoe Company's store. In the 1960s and early 1970s, Mutual Savings and Loan Company had offices there. In the mid-1970s the site began its career as a book store: first as the original Book Mark site, then the Welsh Dragon and now the Book Garden, owned since 2006 by Richard Templeman, below.

113-115 South Main Street was Gittleman's women's clothing store when this picture was taken in 1980. The building's ground level has been Kroger's first Mt. Pleasant Store, Milloy Electric Service, M. J. Murphy's 5 & 10 cent store, Bickley's Music, Hall of Heros, and in 2010 Vision of Performing Arts dance studio. The upstairs has also been busy as home to Dr. Richardson's dental office, Chippewa Lanes bowling alley and the corporate headquarters of the Giant Super Market chain.

117 South Main Street – The New Yorker is downtown Mt. Pleasant's oldest continually operating retail store with the same family ownership. Over the 73 years the store has been open, four generations of shoppers

have passed through the doors. When asked if he had any old pictures of the exterior of the New Yorker children's clothing store, 2010 owners Jack and Trudy Karr said "It hasn't really changed that much." Les and Marjorie Karr opened the doors at this location in 1937, far right building in 1930s street scene, left. In its beginning days the New Yorker specialized in women's and children's clothing, changing in 1975 to strictly childrenswear. Other than updating styles, little has changed here, including the friendly Karr welcome, a New Yorker tradition.

121 South Main Street is the home of Motorless Motion, a well accoutered bicycle shop in space variously occupied by Richmond Shangle Hardware, a Western Auto store, D & D Health Foods store and Mother-To-Be Maternity Shop. Upstairs, in what are apartments in 2010, dentist Dr. E. A. Northway practiced into the 1950s and the Isabella County Department of Welfare had offices.

123 South Main Street has been a bar for about as long as it has been a building. In the 1910s and 1920s it was the Transport Bar, in honor of the Mt. Pleasant-built Transport Truck. In the 1940s through the 1970s, it was first Cascarelli Brothers, then just Cascarelli's as Andy stayed on and Joe went into the travel agency business. In the 1980s it became, as it is in 2010, Marty's Bar, when it was acquired by Martin Naumes. A longtime favorite eatery of those who admire a well priced, well served New York strip steak or fish dinner, Marty's enjoys a good following.

120 South Main Street – This is Cindy Neal's Mole Hole gift shop, here since the 1990s. Cindy and volunteers keep flowering plants tended in most of Mt. Pleasant's public places, including the controversial pedestrian crosswalk islands installed by the Michigan Highway Department on South Mission Street and West High Street. The first Mole Hole gift shop in Mt. Pleasant was located at 217 South Main Street, below in 1980, the second Mt. Pleasant Fire Hall, inset.

122-128 South Main, above, was the site of the 1904 installation of Mt. Pleasant's first cement sidewalk. Note the horse-drawn, steam-powered cement mixer. For orientation purposes, starting left to right in 2010; the building signed "Provisions" is now the northern street front of the Brass Café; the "Meat & Groceries" storefront is now Mt. Pleasant Memories"; the "P. Corey Taylor – Drugs, Wallpaper, Stationery, Books" front, established in 1888, is now Ombodies; and the unsigned building, right, is now The Upper Cut. Below, apparently foot and carriage traffic approved of the South Main curb and sidewalk improvements.

122-124 South Main Street – The Hobby Shop and Isabella Coin Exchange are shown occupying two storefronts on South Main Street in 1988. Ernest Lynn and Valerie Wolters moved their Hobby Shop to this much larger location in 1976. The vacant building on the right would become the Mole Hole of 2010, while the 122 would become the Upper Cut hair salon and 124 Ombodies women's style shop.

127-131 South Main Street – Nickels seems like a great name for a 5, 10 and 50 cent store and Mertz knew a good thing when he saw it. This 1918 photo shows their business in what would in 2010 be the Main Street Professional Center office complex. We'll be back here in a couple pages.

128-130 South Main Street – The above 1982 view of the northwest corner of Main and Michigan Streets provides a glimpse down Michigan Street, left, of the former Kinney wholesale building, a remnant of the Gase Bakery in the 200 block of South Washington. In the forefront, at 130, left, is the storefront that was Donderos Grocery, Wakefields Grocery, later becoming Sisters 3 in the early 1980s and Off Broadway, later, both women's clothing stores, in the late 1980s. To the right of Sister's 3 is the doorway to the Brass Saloon, occupying the space once Chamberlain Brothers, Spagnuola Grocery, Bill Beckett's Grocery, and Bill's Party Take-out. Below, both addresses are occupied by the Brass Café, shown here with the sidewalk in front crowded with the crowd awaiting the appearance of the Budweiser Clydesdale horse team when Fabiano Brothers, Inc. brought the team to Mt. Pleasant May 20, 2010, in celebration of the firm's 125th Anniversary.

127-131 South Main – The building was erected in 1930 by merchant N. D. Gover, whose clothing and general merchandise store moved in from it's East Broadway location. The northeast corner of Main and Michigan streets was later an A & P store, and then the Glen Oren store, above, in 1965, until the late-1970s.

127-131 South Main (continued) – A Glen Oren tradition was each holiday season to select children of needy families to enjoy a shopping spree in the dry goods, shoe, toy and Boy Scout equipment store. Above, in the 1940s, Oren employee Shirley Bragg smiles as the kids show off

their selections. Bragg, who died in 2007, was well known for his work with custom window treatments for Oren's and later for Our Place. He was also active in Michigan railroading history, the Shepherd Depot Museum, and the Isabella County Historical Society. In 2010, the location is the Main Street Professional Center office building.

201 South Main Street - The sign to the left of the door at the far right of the Carpenter Building proclaims this as the first home of the Central Michigan Business Institute and Normal School, see Chapter Seven. Before the building burned to the ground in 1990s, the ground floor, shown above as Simmons Jewelry in 1981, was variously home to Mt. Pleasant Drug Store, Stewart McIntosh Photography, a senior hospitality corner, and a public access local independent television station, last occupant before the fire. The corner in 2010 is host to a flower garden box, maintained by the Mole Hole's Cindy Neal and other volunteers.

201 South Main Street - In 1974, a senior citizens Hospitality Corner opened here, with the sign hanging by Carl Bragg and Leo Bowen witnessed by: third from left in back - City Manager Larry Collins, fifth left in the hat - Zonta President Mrs. Harold Elliott, holding the ladder – Mt. Pleasant Mayor Dean Eckersley and others of the crowd of 75 Zonta members and other area senior citizens

202-218 South Main – In 1948, the west side of the 200 block of South Main Street, above, was occupied by: 202 - a Standard gasoline filling station, 206 – a beauty and barber shop, 208 - Thayer Dairy Bar. Baker Maxwell Walton and fireman Chief Ormond Flynn lived in apartments upstairs over Thayer's; and 218 - the Ward Theater. A Divco milk truck moves south in the lower right quadrant. Nearly 60 years later, in August of 2007, milk truck aficionado Mt. Pleasant's John Straight used his own 1964 Divco milk truck to duplicate the scene down to the vehicle in front of the theater, a rare 2002 Japanese American Isuzu Vehi-Cross.

226 South Main Street – The site was a Shell, then a City's Service gasoline station in the 1920s, both managed by Charles Hall. It was then a small stucco building with no inside bays two open cement pits for auto servicing. Hickcock Oil of Toledo, Ohio, built the present building in 1930. It was a Hi-Speed gas station in those days, above, complete with the Hi-Speed "tower" and decked out in white with green trim. Various managers succeeded including a Rademaker, Pete Mogg and Bob Lamont. At the right is the Ward Theater and just behind the station is the Gase Bakery, home of Old Home Bread, which was demolished and the lot purchased by the City of Mt. Pleasant, who converted it to a 33 car paved parking lot in 1956.

In 1960, Dale and Beryl Sandel bought the station from Bob Lamont and renamed it Sandel's Pure Service Station. After Dale's death in 1974, Beryl continued running the station with the help of Chuck Freeborn and Red McNeal. In 1975, Beryl's son Dale Wayne bought the station and Beryl retired. Red McLean bought the station later and in 2010 is still at the helm, below, the tower and the bays still there, gasoline pumps gone for a decade.

The 200 block of South Main, east side in 1950 was occupied by: 201-Mt. Pleasant Drug; 205- Union Telephone Company; 209 – Household Appliance; 211 - Van's Model Bakery; 213 – Bourland Radio Sales & Service; 215 - City Fire Station; 219 - American Cleaners; 221 – Neff & DeBel Shoe Rebuilding; 223 – Flamingo Bar; 225 – Moose Club; Lynch's Grocery; and 227 – Leo Beard Hy Speed Station.

In 2010, the occupancy is: 201 - vacant lot; 205-209 - Kerr Law Firm and Kerr Parkinsall; 211 - 213 – Main Frame; 215- Blue in the Face; 219 - JoJo's Junk Shop; 223-Bird Bar & Grill; 225- and 227 - Listening Ear.

109 Locust Street - Physician Dr. P. E. Richmond's home was called "one of the neatest of modern residences in the city" when built early in the late 1800s. Dr. Richmond was born in 1846 in Louisville, New York, and began teaching in rural schools there when he was 16. He graduated the medical school at University of McGill in 1873 and set up practice in Mt. Pleasant shortly afterward, having answered the city's call for physicians. He married Anna Gray here in 1877. Dr. Richmond died in 1910. In 2010, the property is completely surrounded by a high cedar hedge, having grown several feet since the photo below was taken in 1990.

304 South Washington was the scene of a 50th Anniversary ice cream social celebration in 1925 for Mr. and Mrs. Frank A. Sweeney. After a luncheon and program for fifty members of the family at the Park Hotel, the party moved to the south lawn of Sweeney's South Washington Street home. Their first home had been over Sweeney's store at 114 South Main Street.

Longtime members of Sacred Heart Catholic Church, the Sweeney's counted several priests among their party guests: Rev. John A. Mulvey and Rev. J. J. Kucinski of Sacred Heart; Rev. Frank Morrison of Clare; Rev. John Fons of Vernon; Rev. Raymond Sweeney of Grand Rapids, a nephew; Rev. William McCann of Alma; Rev. Edward O'Hara of Saginaw; and Rev. James Flannery of Grand Rapids.

Of their six daughters and two sons, two daughters had perished, Eva in 1894 and Mary Ellen in 1922. Immediate family at the anniversary dinner were: Mr. and Mrs. Robert Kane (Cloris Sweeney) and their three sons _ Phil, Gene and John; daughters Mary Lousie, Frances, Marjorie, Bernice, Anna Marie and Roberta. Mr. and Mrs. Frank J. Sweeney (son) and their three children – Bobbie, Dorothy and Bill; and son Dr. Joseph Sweeney of Detroit with daughters Rose Blanid and Kathleen

Besides family, attendees included John, Margaret, Mollie, and Rose Gallagher of Strathroy, Canada, relatives of Mrs. Sweeney from the town where the celebrants met and married prior to Frank A.'s coming to Michigan in 1878 and Mt. Pleasant in 1881.

In 2010, the house stands, minus the porch trellis just removed.

300 South Main Street - Ella Getchell stands in front of the home she shared with husband Dr. Albert T. Getchell when they first came to Mt. Pleasant. Originally from West Falls New York, where he was born in 1856, Getchell came to Michigan when he was 18 years old. In 1877, he married Ella Scoutten of Clio, Michigan, and in 1884 he graduated from the University of Michigan Medical School. He practiced medicine in Grand Rapids and Alma, Michigan, before finding the home above and moving into the large house with room for his medical practice, which thrived because of its proximity to downtown. Below in 2010, the house is and has been for many years, an apartment house.

311 South Main Street - The First Presbyterian Church of Mt. Pleasant began on Court Street with a building just about where the parking lot is on the south side of Mosher Street in 2010. This church at the northeast corner of Main and Wisconsin streets, built for $12,000 in 1907, served the congregation until 1958 when a new church was built at 1250 Watson Road.

400 South Main Street - The replacement of the original Methodist Episcopal Church building, later just Methodist, inset above, by a modern structure at the same address, above, is dealt with severely by Bernie Bonnell in Chapter 20 and needs no further illumination here.

401 South Pine Street – The inset of this photo of Jesse Landon and his wife in front of the family home, above, shows Jesse's father John T. Landon tending his garden at the ornate residence. John T. came to Chippewa Township, Isabella County at age 22 from his native Canada in September, 1862. He worked a year for $15 a month and board for he and his wife. In 1863, he went into debt to buy 40 acres and in 1873, now a prominent landowner, lumberman and farmer, he built the county's first brick structure as a Chippewa Township residence. He was living in this house when he died in 1912, one of 6 properties he owned in Mt. Pleasant.

The house was restored in the 1990s and in 2010 retains the charm of the original home.

CHAPTER 2:DOWNTOWN
LOOKING EAST ON BROADWAY FROM MAIN STREET

East Broadway Street has long been a favorite view of downtown, even before photography was widely used. The two views on this page are from vintage postcards. Views on the following pages are a kaleidoscope of the passage of the years, about which we will let the nature of the street, the evolution of storefronts, and the nature of transporatation illustrate changes in time. We will not designate years in this "slideshow of time", since specifying years has sometimes placed the author in jeopardy with car buffs who are quick to point out "hey, you said that was 19--, when that's a 19-- different year parked right there on the street." So to keep everybody, including automobile enthusiasts, serene, we present East Broadway across the ages without narrative.

Views from the Middle of the 100 block of East Broadway looking east. The spot where the Marianne Shop is at the left of the photo below is the boarded-up lot at the left of the photograph, above. In the 1940s, the 123 East Broadway location was opened as an IGA grocery store, later to be Foland Optical Company, the Marianne Shop, Mr. Charlies and, in 2010, the Trillium, a women's wear store.

LOOKING WEST ON EAST BROADWAY TOWARD MAIN

The second-most favored view of downtown Mt. Pleasant by photographers in all ages seems to have been East Broadway looking west. Originally Broadway ended at Washington Street, until 1874 when the village bought the land of Col. Mosher and pushed west with Broadway to the Chippewa River and further,see West Side Chapter. In the top photo, right, is the Bennett Hotel. In the bottom photo, left, note just left and above the car at the curb is the marquee of the Vaudette Theater, which was bought from Charles Carnahan by Bert Ward, who moved the venue two doors east (taller building), who added a screen named the new theater the Broadway.

Downtown Car Shows - In 1918, above, Martin Naumes of Naumes-Bamber Motor Sales displayed his stock of 1918 Dodge automobiles four abreast and eight deep in the 100 block of East Broadway. Naumes sold cars until his 1938 death. His son Bernard had Naumes Motor Sales at 200 North Mission, which became Hartman Motors, Burgers, and is now Shaheen Motors. Fifteen years later, center, Clarence Hart displayed his inventory in front of his dealership in the 200 block of West Broadway.

Nineteen years after that, E. Lee Johnson from his dealership over at the corner of Michigan and College streets, organized his 1952 and 1953 Studebakers to caravan a band trip to Holland, Michigan.

Not pictured here is the Leo Beard Lincoln Mercury dealership at Main and Illinois nor Krapohl Ford on Court Street.

In 2010, no downtown car dealerships exist.

100 East Broadway – In 1876, it was the Enterprise Building, above, with Doughty Brothers mercantile and the Enterprise newspaper and printing offices having located there after the great fire across Broadway in 1875. Next door to the west was Carr & Granger Drugs, with a meeting hall upstairs which served as an entertainment venue prior to the opera house a block away later. Over time the building housed Marsh & Lewis Mercantile, then the Exchange Bank, was built on the site in 1907, right. After a number of name changes including American Security Bank and National City Bank, the building is vacant in 2010, having been vacated by National City Bank in favor of what is perceived to be a more central location.

101-103 East Broadway – The building at the far left of this 1988 photograph above is probably one of the oldest continually used buildings in downtown Mt. Pleasant. It was built as the wood frame Fancher business block by village pioneer Isaac A. Fancher in 1873 and was the place where the fire of 1875 started. It has variously been the home of Gover's Clothing Store until 1931, the D & C Store, Lloyd's Footwear and is now Downtown Discount Party Store and sister store Downtown Dollar, below.

105 East Broadway Street – In 1978, Bill and Eva Mourtzouhos, above with nephew Mike Sarakatsonis, bought the Downtown Restaurant, Mt. Pleasant's oldest downtown restaurant . The Mourtzouhos had previously owned the Chicken Shack at 601 North Mission from 1965 to 1975

before selling to Lester Thelan. Bill came to United States from Greece in the mid 1950s and was living in Chicago where he met Eva visiting relatives there. He followed her back to Mt. Pleasant and they were married in 1958. They retired in 1997, right. The restaurant remained the Downtown for a few years before becoming Larabee's Family Restaurant. In 2010, the Midori Sushi Bar is due to open at the thoroughly remodeled location by year's end.

121-123 East Broadway – The occasion of the above photo is vague but it is probably a holiday street sing, which was common in earlier years. . Note girl in the far right dressed as an elf. In the background is the north side of the street, left to right; 121 East Broadway - Evenknit Hosiery, later Fashion City women's clothing, now Downtown Drugs; 123 – Mr. Charlie's women's apparel, the Trillium in 2010; and 125 – Tuma's Farm Market, later Scully's Jewelry, now Max & Emily's Bakery Café. In earlier days, 123 East Broadway was the site of Thad Hayling and Dan Johnson's meat market, later Johnson and Honeywell Meat Market. .Below, actor-songster-guitarist Jeff Daniels performs August 21, 2010, in the street in front of Max & Emily's and Trillium to a crowd of more than 2,300 as part of the eatery's annual street concert series started in 2009 by Max & Emily's, Isabella Bank and Downtown Mt. Pleasant.

200 East Broadway - Isabella Bank began as Isabella County State Bank in 1903 when industrialist/banker John Weidman, who had started the Weidman State Bank the year before, bought a private bank at 200 East Broadway and renamed it. The building included the opera house upstairs where traveling shows performed and where rural school graduation ceremonies were held.

The building changed little for many years, as seen below in the 1940s.

Isabella Bank (continued) the main bank underwent a major facelift in the late 1970s with aluminum cladding attached to the building. The bank continued expanding to the east leading up to the remodeling, which bound acquired storefronts into a contiguous building image. In 2009, the Isabella Bank moved its main office and administration functions to 401 North Main Street. In 2010, the building, as an office building, is home to the Mt. Pleasant Chamber of Commerce, Mt. Pleasant Visitors and Convention Bureau, and Middle Michigan Development.

Isabella Bank (continued) Meantime, across the street on the north side of Broadway, Isabella Bank had replaced the Grants store, built on the site of the Ben Franklin store that had been erected following the demolition of the Hotel Bennett at 139 East Broadway, with its main banking branch in the 1970s. Isabella County State Bank evolved into Isabella Bank and Trust and finally just Isabella Bank, while expanding offices and services office housing westward. Isabella Bank offices now extend from the corner of Court and Broadway streets through the Someplace Special Hallmark Card and gift shop storefront at 137 East Broadway, the Dittman's building at 133 East Broadway and the Economy 5 & 10 cent store building, later Gay's 5 & 10 at 129-131 East Broadway, to in 2010 be immediately adjacent to Max & Emily's Bakery and Café at 125 East Broadway, below.

205 East Broadway was the site of the short-lived teenage and Central student entertainment venue featuring dancing, musical entertainment and non-alcoholic refreshments. Peggie Fuller, later to be Peggie Edmonds is holding the totem pole in the left photo, above, with her friend Mavis Hagerman is, bracing Peggie in the left photo and peeking from inside the teepee in the right photo. They preserved their memories of their favorite place for themselves, and fortunately us, in 1943. Thanks to Peggie Edmonds for sharing this rare shot of one of Mt. Pleasants favorite teenage icons of the 1940s.

The site was later home to Belle's Hat Shoppe, El Cove and now is the Broadway entrance to the Blue Gator, still a gathering place for slightly older youth.

214 East Broadway Street - One of Mt. Pleasant's most fascinating "humble beginnings to business empire" stories is that of Fabiano Brothers Inc. They began as a fruit market on East Broadway and became the state's largest beverage distributor, now headquartered in Bay City after a consolidation of facilities in Mt. Pleasant and Saginaw.

The story begins with Gennaro Fabiano, who opened a "cantina" in San Ippolito, Italy, in 1885, selling fruit, vegetables and his own homemade wine. The cantina is still being operated by Fabiano distant relatives. Gennaro came to the United States and worked for the railroad in Missouri to earn money to bring his wife and family to America, where they settled in Eaton Rapids, Michigan, and opened a fruit market in 1911. They opened a new store and moved to Lansing in 1915. When

relatives in Mt. Pleasant perished in an influenza epidemic, orphaning four of Gennaro's grandchildren, he moved his family and business operations here in 1919 so that he could raise those children in their familiar environment. Fabiano and his two sons, Frank A. and Joseph R. established a retail and wholesale store, Fabiano Fruit Market, at 214 East Broadway, left, where Headliners is located in 2010.

In making the trip to Detroit's Eastern Market for their store and wholesale customers, the Fabiano's picked up distribution rights for Stroh Near Beer in its two county territory in 1923 when Prohibition curtailed their wine business. In 1930, Gennaro died, leaving Frank and Joe the business. In 1933, Prohibition was repealed and the Stroh Brewery distribution had grown, so Fabiano's moved to a Franklin Street warehouse and began a distribution relationship with Anheuser-Busch. The Franklin Street warehouse was destroyed by fire in 1965 and the business moved to 1213-1219 North Mission Street, where they incorporated in 1969. In 1977, Frank A. died and James Fabiano, son of Joseph R., was appointed president of the company. Continued expansions and acquisitions have continued and Fabiano. Inc. employs hundreds of people in a distribution area covering nearly all the Michigan Lower Peninsula.

In 2010, the 125th Anniversary of Gennaro Fabiano's founding of the base company, Fabiano's brought the Budweiser Clydesdale horses to Mt. Pleasant to celebrate, and provide this book with a great cover.

300 block East Broadway – The Taylor Building, once home to Bride's Beautiful, Taylor's Sunoco Service, Sun Oil Company, attorneys T. R. and J. R. McNamara, Chapman Oil and City's Service Oil Company Production Department, shown above after a devastating 1988 fire that led to the buildings demolition, was the anchor of the south side of the 300 block of East Broadway. The block hosted such businesses as the One Minute Lunch, Sam's Shoe Repair, Star Beauty and Barber Shop and the Church of Christ, Homes by Kirsch and at 319 then and now, Mutual Savings and Loan since the 1970s. Below, the block in 2010 is occupied only by a medical practice and Mutual.

300 East Broadway, the Hersee Building over the years was business home to a diverse number of business entities including, above in 1982, the Mt. Pleasant Chamber of Commerce, which has been housed over Dittman's Store at 133 East Broadway, at 120 East Broadway, in the old J. C. Penny building at 114 East Broadway and finally, in 2010, one of a suite of offices including the Mt. Pleasant Area Convention & Visitors Bureau and Middle Michigan Development Corporation in the original Isabella County State Bank building at the southeast corner of Broadway and University streets, 200 East Broadway.

Other business occupants of the Hersee Building before it burned March 8, 2004, below, were: Montgomery Ward, the Isabella County Herald and, upstairs, dozens of oil and gas exploration and production entities including I. W. "Bucky" Hartman, John Neyer, Fred Turner, Dick Wolcott and Bill Strickler to name just a handful.

304 East Broadway - In 1989, the staff of Mt. Pleasant Realty posed for an ad wishing Mt. Pleasant a happy 100th Anniversary of the village's designation as a city. Left to right is: Ed Moe, Keith Feight, Rick Arlt, Mike Wing, Connie Ososki, Jerry McFarlane, Joyce Arndt, Doug Schutte, Andrea Wilson, Robin Stressman, Linda Partlo, Jack Neyer, Sally Wilson, Russ Kelley, Judi West, Julia Pulcifer, Marge Mills, Randy Golden, and Sue White. Not pictured were: Gene Knight, Doug McFarlane, Doris Sherwood, Judy Pape, Sue Monroe, Vickie Castro, Ann Voss, Don Voss, and Pete Alexander. Below, Mt. Pleasant Realty in 2010, in the building constructed in 2004 after the 2004 fire that destroyed their Hersee Building home, previous page.

306 East Broadway – In the 1950s, local schoolchildren decorated downtown windows for Halloween including the Michigan Consolidated Gas Building. Note the Taylor Building reflected in the window. The "for rent" storefront in the Hersee Building next door would become the home of Mt. Pleasant Realty, previous page. Following the 2004 fire next door, building owners Tolas Oil & Gas remodeled and in 2010 the building is home to the Tolas Enterprises, petroleum geologist Charles Moskowitz, the Winters law firm and Partlo Property Management.

100 block South University – On August 7, 1949, soundings were taken for soil sampling to test the soils integrity for placing the footings of the new Mt. Pleasant Municipal Building, completed in 1950. Business along the block at the time included Western Union, Enterprise Print Shop, Women's Exchange Thrift Shop, Hal's Tots N Teens, attorney Ray Markel, Stinson Agency and Dr. Baskerville. In 2010, businesses include Emma's women's fashions, Benefit Consulting, Central Insurance Agency, Flexible Health & Wellness, Scrubs & Such, Ross Accounting and attorneys Stein & Higgs and Janes, Backus & Janes.

120 South University – In 1887, when this was Church Street, the Mt. Pleasant Fire Department was headquartered on the corner of Michigan and Church Streets, replacing a Methodist Church that previously stood here.

The Fire Department moved to the 200 block of South Main Street. In 1950, the Fire Department returned to the corner when the Mt. Pleasant Municipal Building was built, with expanded fire truck housing. In 2010, below, the structure is now the Basin Building, the address is that of Crystal Computer Support.

302 South University Street – The base cobblestone structure law office complex was built in 1901 by a lady believed to be Mt. Pleasant's first female medical doctor, Dr. Amy Holcomb, who had the building designed to accommodate her medical practice. The 1948 Mt. Pleasant City directory shows the property owned by a O. Holcomb, likely a descendent. By 1963, the Michigan Department of Corrections shared the building with owner Realtor George J. Marks. In 1981, Andrew Marks sold the building to attorney Tim Taylor, who converted an upstairs apartment to his office. In 1987, above, Taylor added a 3,500 square foot wing to the building, then co-owned with attorney Tom Hall, Jr., and then the building was home to the legal practices of Taylor, Daniel Pyscher, Daniel O'Neil, Hall, John Lewis, Paul Chamberlain and William T. Ervin.

In 2010, right, the Cornerstone Professional Center home to the offices of attorneys Beck Bolles, Tom Hall Jr., Lesley Hoenig, Jeffrey Lynch, Daniel O'Neil and Daniel H. Pyscher.

The 1880s Mount Pleasant Women's Club, a force to be reckoned with, was the nucleus of what was to evolve as the Mt. Pleasant Library system. Pictured is the group about the time the 1879 Library, Literary and Musical Association was organized. Left to right: back row – Mrs. Fred Taylor, Mrs. Harold Chatterton, Mrs. Wells Brown, Mrs. Cockran, Hester McNutt, Mrs. Newberry, unidentified, Mrs. A. R. Gorham, Arminta Kelly, Mrs. Bennett, Mrs. Herb Sanford, Lizzie Foster; center row - Lois Wilson, Nan Northway, unidentified, Mrs. Dusenbury, Mrs. Fred Keeler, Mrs. Dodds, Virgilene Collins, Hannah Vowles; front row - unidentified, Mrs. Blanche Maybee, Mrs. Sheline, Mrs. Carey Taylor, Mrs. Tom Battle and Mabel Doughty.

In 1909, the Mt. Pleasant Women's Club established a public library, first in the Main Street offices, then to an East Broadway home, below.

301 South University - The Mt. Pleasant Public Library finally located in the First Congregational Society, previously the Unitarian Society, building, above, at the southeast corner of Illinois and Normal Street, the 2010 location of Veterans Memorial Library. By 1953, the past forty years of library user traffic had taken its toll on the old white wood frame building. And the city began to examine funding and design of a new library, which was put into service May 24, 1957, dedicated to Mt. Pleasant's veterans of all wars. The author is grateful to local historian/genealogist Sherry Sponseller for her research on the library's history for its 100th birthday.

301 South University (continued) - The Mt. Pleasant Library Board and City Commission approved plans for the new $90,000 public library at their July 16, 1956, meeting. Shown above reviewing the plans, left to right are: City Manager Allen Kronbach, architect Elmer Black, Mayor G. R. "Rollie" Denison, Board Chairman Charles W. McKenzie, architect Edward White, Commissioner Helen Johnson, Librarian Elsa Struble, City Attorney Edward N. Lynch, Commissioner Lou Johnson, Commissioner Joe Rush and Library Board Member J. D. Marcus. Below, the cornerstone for the new library was laid November 26, 1956, at 301 South College.

301 South University (continued) - The November 26, 1956, Mt. Pleasant Public Library cornerstone laying is shown, above, being mortared by Lola Benford, while Mayor G. R. Denison, Clessie Houghtaling, J. D. Marcus, City Manager Allan Kronbach, Library Board Chairman Dr. Charles W. Mackenzie and Librarian Elsa Struble look on. Below, the completed library adjoins the foundation of the wooden structure that served as the library from 1924 until demolition in 1956.

301 South University (continued) – In 1974, the library was feeling space limitation strain as not just books but the need for computer services continued to grow. Voters approved a $1.2 million bond to expand the library into the building used in 2010.

When the Mt. Pleasant Post Office relocated to a new facility at the corner of Main and Pickard streets in 2002, the Illinois Street building, across the alley to the east of the library and the land it sat on became available, a rare opportunity to gain much needed library space. The Mt. Pleasant Library Board bought the former post office building and renovated it just enough to make the building usable for library purposes, attached that building to the library with a walkway across the vacated alley, and named it the Library Annex, below.

In 2008, voters rejected a planned library expansion and in 2009 remodeling was done to re-contour the use of the limited space available. Renovation was completed in time to celebrate the 100th Birthday of the Mt. Pleasant Library.

Space and equipment needs continue to plague the ability of the library to fully serve. For that reason, a portion of the proceeds from the sale of this book will be dedicated to buying updated microfilm reading equipment for the Veteran's Memorial Library.

100 block of East Michigan Street in 2010 is anchored on the east side by an Isabella Bank drive-in branch, above left, and the former City Hall, now the Basin Building, below right. Over the years, companies that have occupied this block are: 107 – grocers Johnson & Fisher and William Mindel; 108 – optometrist James C. Freeman and tailor Frank Schmidt; 109 - Fish Brothers bicycle shop and barber Bill Edmonds; 110 - Pleasant Answering Service, Robinson Appliance Service, and Scully Jewelry; 111 - The Upper Cut; 113- Michigan Meat Market; 114 – Freeman Dairy, followed by Northland Dairy; 118- attorney Fred Wallington; 124 – Union Cab and Bus Terminal, barber Patrick Karns, barber Bill Edmonds, Milady's Barber & Beauty Shop and Lymar Beauty Shop; and 130 - Johnson Motor Sales.

130 East Michigan – The southwest corner of Michigan Street at Normal, now University Street never could figure out what address was correct for the business. It was the site of a Johnson organization from 1915, above, until 1963. Floyd Johnson first opened Johnson's Garage in 1915 and was, at various stages, an Allis Chalmers tractor dealer, a Ford Motors dealer and ultimately a Studebaker car dealer before his 1947 death. In the above photo, looking east along Michigan Street, sees Sacred Heart Academy in the background, Johnson's is seen as a one story Ford dealer. Below, Floyd and staff pose between the gas pumps for an ad promoting Iso Vis Motor Oil.

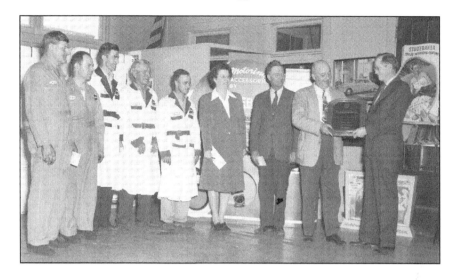

130 East Michigan (continued) – In 1947, Floyd Johnson dies and his son E. Lee Johnson became president of Johnson Motors,, which thrived with him the helm. The company earned a Studebaker Sales Award in 1948, above, Present for the award, left to right, were Johnson employees: Art Graham, Ralph Bellinger, Woody Reed, Al Albright, Charlie Barrett, Florence Mullins, Norm Hayward, an unnamed Studebaker District Manager and E. Lee Johnson. Below, 41-year Johnson Motors veteran Art Graham and Service Manager Charlie Barrett check out the snappy new 1957 Studebaker.

130 East Michigan (continued) – Before the last Studebakers rolled off the assembly line at the home plant in South Bend, Indiana, the fate of Johnson Motors was sealed. Losing the Studebaker brand and with other major motor companies already represented in Mt. Pleasant, the likelihood of sustaining the operation on repairs alone was not in the cards and the business closed. The building was torn down in 1963 to make room for an Isabella County State Bank drive-up branch, still in operation in 2010 as a branch of Isabella Bank.

200 block of East Michigan Street in 2010 has only one business address, that being Bob's Barber Shop at 211 East Michigan, above,. Bob's is owned and operated by founder Bob Cook's son Bill Cook, a busy volunteer fireman and young father who somehow hasn't gotten around to changing the name of the business since his dad retired more than a decade ago.

The only other occupants of 200 block of East Michigan, on the south side in 2010, are the north perimeter of the old post office building property, shown above in the 1940s with the Delphine LaFromboise home next door to the south, later the offices of real estate developer Phil Sybert before late 1990s destruction for a city parking lot extension. The post office building, alter the Mt. Pleasant Public Schools Administration offices and in 2010 an office building, has changed little since 1925 construction and is listed in the National Historic Register. The rest of the south side of the 200 block is the site of Sacred Heart Academy Elementary School.

100 Block of South Franklin Street – In 1948, this block was business home to: 100 – R. J. Hersee office, Turner Petroleum Company, Gordon Oil Company, R. H. Butterfield, Stewart Oil Company, attorney R. Lee Browning, M. Osgood, Lincoln Drilling, and geologist Ole Kristofferson; 106 – O. O. Long, Scott Westbrook; 108 - Struble Barber Shop; 115- Roy's Magneto and 117 - the Stumac Restaurant. In later years, Enterprise Printers and Mt. Pleasant's first Dairy Queen soft ice cream walk-up store would occupy the northeast corner of Franklin and Michigan Streets. In 2010, the 100 block of South Franklin is occupied by 115 – Behavioral Medicine Associates, CPA Dan Dedloff, Mt. Pleasant Agency Insurance and Valley Travel Company.

300 block of East Michigan and East Illinois streets – The first Roman Catholic church in Mt, Pleasant was St. Charles, a wood frame building built in 1875 on three acres in the 300 block of Oak Street about where Oak Street apartments are located in 2010, presided by Father John McCarthy, who died in 1885. The new pastor, Father James Crowley, seeing the parish grow more rapidly than the church could accommodate, purchased the 300 block of East Michigan for the princely sum of $1,500 in 1887, seen above looking southeast from the corner of Church, now University, and Illinois streets, moving the old wood frame chuch to that location and setting about building a new church, above. The new church, built for $25,000, opened in 1889 with a new name, Sacred Heart, and the old wood church had a second floor added to it, left, and became Sacred Heart Academy. Note the inset above of 1950s repair being performed on the steeple. The priests residence was built in 1895. Below, in 2010, the entire property is occupied by the Sacred Heart Parish Hall, Sacred Heart Academy school and gym.

300 block of East Michigan and East Illinois streets (continued), and 300 South Fancher street – Looking northwest from the corner of Illinois and Lansing streets, the Sacred Heart Catholic Church, parsonage and school is seen in 1906. The school was replaced by a brick structure in 1908, next page. The church/rectory configuration worked for several decades until enrollment of Sacred Heart Academy and the moving of Mt. Pleasant High School, to the southeast outer reaches of town on Elizabeth Street, caused the need to expand the Academy's physical plant with a new elementary school building, gym and parish hall taking the place of the church and parsonage above.

The entire complex moved exactly one block east and just a touch to the south in 1970, below, with an almost identical juxtaposition of church and administative buildings, below, in the 300 block of South Fancher Street. The former rectory in the foreground is all offices and meeting rooms in 2010, with the priest/parson residing in a parish-bought home at 1009 South Kinney.

The Sacred Heart Catholic Church 1935 First Communion Group consisted of, left to right: First row – Mary Ann Lasko, Charlotte Campbell, Teresa Hickey, Mary M. Bronstetter, Audrey Smith, Lillian Fortino, Kathleen Strauss, Margaret L. Lowther, Joan Sova, Madonna L. Kirkey, and Ann Hackett.

Second row – William McDonell, Ronald Doerr, James Lenon, Walter Heintz, John Walker, Joseph Cascarelli, William Sheppard, John Hagan, Edward Anderson, Norbert Hall, Robert Fate, Gerald Murphy, Thomas R. McNamara, William Sweeney, James Campbell, Stanley Dole, Robert Davis, and Glenn Voisin.

Third row – Mary Bechtel, Marie Anderson, Elizabeth Hackett, Mary J. Cuthbert, Charles A. Deibel, Paul Fortino, Thomas Horvath, Raymond McNamara, Thomas Powell, William Eckert, Robert Evans, Leona Windel, Catherine Keller, Virginia Torpey, Anna Marie Mahaffey.

Fourth row – Mary Louise McCarthy, Mary Wadolowski, Helen Szekeres, Rose Ellen Quillen, Joan Moeller, Erlinda Rodriquez, Joseph Rodrequez, Ladisloa Wadlowski, Margaret Fortino, Ruth L. Ball and Elizabeth McDonald.

The author is grateful for the photo, above, to Mt. Pleasant's Joe Cascarelli, right in this photo with an unidentified vintage costumed waitress and his brother Andy at Cascarelli's, 125 South Main, during Mt. Pleasant's village Centennial year of 1967.

300 block of East Michigan (continued) – Sacred Heart Academy's original building was the old St. Charles Catholic Church, Mt. Pleasant's first. The brick building in the postcard view, above, from the collection of the late Richard Brandell, was erected in 1908 and shows students lining up to go to mass at the church immediately behind the school. Note the home at the right, which dates the view to before the Post Office Building was built at the corner of Michigan and Normal Street, a block to the west of the school. Below, in 2010, the 1908 building has been modernized and is surrounded by elementary and high school buildings occupying not only the entire 300 block but half of the 200 block of East Michigan as well.

301 East Chippewa is the oldest remaining house in Mt. Pleasant.
The home was practically new, built about 1865, when the Wilkinson
Doughty family gathered on the front porch, above, to pose for a
photograph with the Doughty Company wagon out in front. Wilkinson
Doughty was a merchant, town trustee, one of the founders of Central
Michigan Normal School, now University. The last Doughty to occupy
the house was Margaret Doughty, below, shown on the same front porch
about a hundred years after her ancestors bought the house in 1869.
Margaret Doughty died in 1993.

301 East Chippewa (continued) is "a carefully preserved example of balloon frame pioneer architecture" according to Michigan Historical Marker #L223A, place on the front of the house on the U.S. Bicentennial July 4th weekend in 1976. Shown above with wooden sidewalks and a dirt Franklin Street running alongside. Note the five chimneys. The house remains, below, in good shape and was used as a bed and breakfast inn for awhile and is now a family residence.

109-117 West Broadway – Looking southeast from the Borden's condensery smokestack in 1910, the steeple in the background is that of Sacred Heart Catholic Church. In the foreground are the buildings along the south side of Broadway to Washington. The "just off Main Street" businesses in the 100 block of West Broadway have over the years included; 109 – Falsetta's first restaurant, Franklin Supply in 1947, Mt. Pleasant Supply in the 1960s through the mid-1970s; 111 - Del's Photo Service in 1947 and the Moose Club from the 1940s to the 1980s; 117 – Bailes Beauty School in 1947 and Mt. Pleasant Beauty School by the 1970s. The beauty school became M. J. Murphy's Beauty School and moved across Washington Street in the mid-1970s. For awhile in the 1970s and 1980s, 117 was the offices of Jay Woods, oil developer.

In 2010, below, the buildings of 100 West Broadway, south side, are occupied by the Faith Community Church.

110 West Broadway – Frank P. Gruss purchased this Standard Oil gasoline filling station, above, from Pat McNerny on Park Hotel land. Frank paid $2,500 for the enterprise and paid a $100 yearly rental fee to the hotel. Francis "Frank" Gruss worked in the station until he was drafted into the army in the autumn of 1945, replaced at the pump by returning veteran Ross Dart. Frank Dart, Sr. owned the station until 1952 and proudly told his son that one of those years he made $5,000. In 2010, the site is part of the Mt. Pleasant Town Center. Left in the background is Calvin Crawford's American Laundry, while the Campbell Building is the darker building at the right. Below, Elmer Jones and Bert Sweet take a break from work at Renwick Mill, with Gruss Standard and the Park Hotel background right.

100 block South Washington Street – Modern downtown snow removal, in the 1940s as in the 21st Century, is handled deftly, swiftly and with much roaring of heavy equipment. This undated scene shows just a glimpse of the businesses on the west side of South Washington. In fact, sign shows at the right for the gasoline filling station for what was Priors Service Station, and would become Shep's Tires, and in 2010 Curts Automotive Repair at 122 South Washington.

The remainder of the block consisted of: 110 – Sweeney Seed Company and 114 Albar Nash. In 2010, below, Sweeney Seed remains and Albar Nash has been replaced by Off Broadway Performing Arts Center.

CHAPTER 3: NORTH END

222 North Fancher Street – Befitting his position as Vice President of Gorham Brothers Co., Mt. Pleasant's largest and most prestigious lumber company and saw mill, Arwin E. Gorham built a huge home at the corner of Fancher and Chippewa Streets, angled to face both and neither. Gorham came to Mt. Pleasant when the company moved its business interests here in 1888. A. E. Gorham married Sarah M. Balmer of Mt. Pleasant in 1891. He was connected with the Exchange Savings Bank, becoming its President in 1905. Mr. Gorham died in 1931. Later the house was torn down and the foundation used as the basis for a brick Cape Cod-style home, enshrouded in trees and exquisite landscaping in 2010, below.

315 North Fancher – The home, above, was once the carriage house for the John Doughty home at 415 East Chippewa, back porch at the left above. In 1949, the widow Wildermuth sold the structure to oilfield drilling contractor Noah Andrews, who introduced rotary drilling rigs to the Michigan oilpatch. Andrews had a white Cape Cod-style home constructed on the property, which remains in pristine condition.

404 North Fancher – Built by one of the Chatterton family in 1919, this tile roofed brick home was owned twice by auto dealer J. F. Battle in 1943 and after taking it back from a land contract later, Battle died and the home became that of oilfield driller William "Billy" Hilliard from 1958 until 1979, when the present owners bought and have continually maintained the historic integrity of the house.

403 North Main Street - The northwest corner of Main and Lincoln, has always been a busy corner as the Horning Grain Elevator did business at the corner, alongside the entrance to what is now Island Park, until 1903 when J. E. and son Howard E. Chatterton left the grocery business and bought the mill, renaming it J. E. Chatterton & Son. The location saw the 1934 opening of Mt. Pleasant's first air conditioned building, The Atha Suppy Company, oil field supply dealer. Atha was later bought by Oilwell Supply Company, who operated at that location until 1986, when the building was demolished.

403 North Main (continued) was the site of the City of Mt. Pleasant governmental offices, moved from 120 South University Avenue in 1986. City offices remained there until November, 2008, when the move was made to new quarters in the newly-reclaimed Borden Building (see chapter entitled "Magificent Comeback on West Broadway" in this book). Since early 2009, the northwest corner of Main and Lincoln have been corporate offices for Isabella Bank.

404 North Main was the location of the Peninsular House, a hotel/boardinghouse built in 1883 and operated by J. N. Vancise at the northeast corner of Lincoln and Main street, across the street from the Main Street entrance to Island Park. Since the conversion to apartments, in 1948, renters of the home were listed as I. L. Herring and and J. N. White. In 2010, the address remains an apartment house.

The Deibels of 221 North Kinney - Mt. Pleasant got a taste of the power of early television in 1954. Chuck and Marge, both 26 were on vacation in New York City in September,1954. Marge was selected from the studio audience to be on-camera with popular CBS television personality Gary Moore. Moore chatted with Marge for a bit, establishing she was a homemaker from Mt. Pleasant, Michigan, husband Chuck sold appliances for Consumers Power Company and there were two Deibel children. They talked about giveaway game shows and how the Gary Moore Show said the gifts his show gave were not charity but were given through sponsors.

Then Moore decided to test the charity of his three million television audience.

On a whim, Moore turned to the camera and said, live, "Why don't we all get together and send Mrs. Deibel some money, just for nothing. Send a nickel to Mrs. Charles Deibel. Let's try it just for fun."

Chuck and Marge Deibel in 1954

The Deibels of 221 North Kinney (continued) - The Deibels returned to Mt. Pleasant to resume what they thought was going to be their normal life. "Two days later," Marge recalls, "the mailman pulled up in front of the house with bags of mail for us. We formally accepted it and had it delivered to city hall, where they put it in the basement and more than 400 came to help us count and bag it over the next two weeks."

Mt. Pleasant Police officer Bob Davis escorts the Deibels from the City Hall to Isabella Bank with a cartload of nickels.

The Deibels of 221 North Kinney (continued) - Over the next couple of weeks the Deibels received more than 120,000 pieces of mail with nickels totaling over $7,800.

For awhile the question of income tax came up but it was ultimately decided that each gift was only a nickel and no tax would be due on a nickel. Never mind there were thousands of them. Besides, it was reasoned, the number of letters sent to the Deibels represented more than $3,600 in stamp revenue to the government … more than the income tax would be on the $7,800.

For many years thereafter, Mt. Pleasant declared itself "The Nickel Capital of the World", until time eroded the meaning of the phrase.

With the proceeds of the nickel adventure, they built a house, had another little Deibel, making three, and moved again. Marge took up a teaching career at Mt. Pleasant High School in 1959 that would last for 25 years and Chuck became Deputy Mt. Pleasant City Clerk in 1956, then City Clerk, a job from which he would retire in 1988. They moved once more, to their present East Broadway address when they became "empty nesters."

In completing this book, the author had the Deibels return to their old address on North Kinney for the "now" part of this saga. They graciously agreed, although the dog that distracted Marge in the 1954 photo has long since gone to his eternal reward as a result of a mishap with a car before the Deibels moved from this

address. Above, meet Chuck and Marge of 2010 on the lawn of the house where they lived when the great nickel adventure happened.

625 North Main Street – The first Mt. Pleasant railroad depot was built on this location in 1879 for a narrow gauge Pere Marquette train track linking the town with Coleman. Following a 1930s fire, the building was sold and moved to 215 Palmer Street. The man in the center, above, is Frank Brownson. A replacement building was later razed and a new office building built in the late 1980s. The present building houses the offices of the Michigan Education Association and Whitford Chiropractic Clinic.

625 North Main Street – Spearheaded by the Mt. Pleasant Area Historical Society in 1987, a community-wide campaign was launched to save the Pere Marquette railroad depot on North Main. A grant was received but the real estate market caused the price of the depot to increase beyond the funds available. The grant was used instead to purchase a home at 623 North Fancher, which served as the Society's headquarters until maintenance costs became prohibitive and the house was sold. The Society still meets, first Tuesday of the month at 7:00 p.m.. at the Isabella County Commission on Aging building on Lincoln Road in 2010. Above, the 1987 officers of the Mt. Pleasant Area Historical Society pose in front of the building they tried in vain to save. Left to right are: President John Cumming, Secretary Ellen Penwell, Vice-President Margaret Doughty and Treasurer Paul Kruska. Not pictured were Board Members Reynolds Campbell, Don Fuller and Mike Hamas.

813 North Main Street has been the home of the U. S. Postal Service in Mt. Pleasant since 2002, above, following sojurns in the 200 block of East Illinois for nearly four decades and at 201 South University, Normal, or College, Street depending on the era, since 1925 before that. In the late 1800s, the property was part of the Leaton and Upton Saw Mill spread.

At the very end of North Main Street is the Michigan Consolidated Gas Company Mt. Pleasant Service and Maintenance office, straddling the 100 East Pickard and 100 West Pickard line. While there is nothing particularly imposing about the building in 2010, centraris resident Bill Burden tells us the location was once the site of a plant that manufactured natural gas. The site may be the site of the Mt. Pleasant Light and Fuel Company, constructed in 1904 far enough from downtown to be safe in case of an explosion.

822 North Main Street – Originally called Otto's Grocery, this store served the role of what we would now call a convenience store. The business was later renamed Frank's Grocery and closed in the early 1980s.

In 2010, the lot is vacant, bracketed to the south by the empty building that housed Ben Traines auto and truck parts and, in the 1930s, was a dealer for Republic trucks. Just east is the Empty Keg Party, formerly named Cheers, store, keeping the corner of Main and Pickard still in the "party store" business.

704-720 North Kinney Street – The original Kinney School was built in the 1800s, inset, named for Mt. Pleasant Pioneer John

Kinney, 1837-1919, came to Mt. Pleasant in 1863 and bought 200 acres northeast of Mt. Pleasant, which would become the Kinney addition to the town in 1878. The original building was replaced by the above modern structure in the 1920s. The building served as an elementary school for many years and in 2010 houses the Mt. Pleasant Child Development Center in the north end and the Mt. Pleasant Public Schools Administrative office in the south end, below.

905 North Kinney Street - An unnamed employee, Harold, Danny, Paul, and Earl Ducommon pose in front of Ducommon Machine Company, above, about 1945. The company specialized in welding and oilfield machinery repair. In the mid-1960s, the business was purchased by Don and Shirley Rise and became Rise Machine Company, below. Rise Machine specializes in oilfield equipment maintenance and repair. Don Rise was the inventor of "The Kicker" a 12 volt engine starter in the 1980s. In 2010, D. J. Rise is president of the company.

Dow Chemical Company once operated a salt works at the very north end of Fancher Street with the plant on the south side of the Chippewa River, above, and property to the north of the river. The property had been purchased from the Isabella County Fair Board and was the site of the county's first fairs, north of the present Lease Management Inc. at the Fancher/Industrial streets corner. When the salt works closed, Dow deeded their property north of the river to the Mt. Pleasant Country Club and the land facing Mission Street became Lee Equipment Company. Below, the site of Indian Mills/Isabella City, Mt. Pleasants "seedling" settlement, is seen at the bridge, right, from the tower of the salt works.

CHAPTER 4: NORTH MISSION STREET

The northwest corner of Broadway at Mission Street was called both 101 North Mission and 720 East Broadway, depending on which reference is used. Either way, Norm Fuller's Standard Service Station was doing well at that location in the mid-1940s, above. Later years would find the location always a Standard Station but with different names. On the same side of the street in the 100 block over the years were: 105 – Henry Littekind, Maxi-Muffler and Michigan Auto Top; 107 – AAA Auto Club of Michigan, Kirby Vacuum Cleaner, Levi's Used Books; and 123-Central State Oil & Gas Service, Stutting's Service Station, and Jerry's Transmission. In 2010, below, the east side of the 100 block of North Mission is taken up by the Rite-Aid Drug Store.

Pauline Howard's brother Henry Neff, Pauline and Ellis Howard pose with children Bob Howard and Rosemary Neff in front of Polly's Market in the 1950s.

116 North Mission Street – Polly's Market began at the northeast corner of Mission Street and Broadway when Ellis Michael Ellis and his wife Pauline "Polly" Howard began selling fruits and vegetables to travelers along Mission, then US Highway 27 in the early 1940s. Diligence and long hours earned the market popularity among travelers and locals as a great place for fresh sausage, eggs and refreshments. Married in 1935 in Miami, Florida, the Howards started Polly's market in 1939 in Pauline's hometown and it grew beyond their dreams, the business often operating 24 hours a day. Ellis Howard was killed in an oil well explosion in 1962, visiting a wellsite in which he had an interest. Traffic and shopping habits with the arrival of expressways and mega-super markets, gradually eroded the business base that had made Polly's successful. The site became the home of Chris's Drive-in and is now the abandoned Sweet Onion Restaurant building, as well as sharing addresses with Shaheens Motor Sales, originally built by Ben Traines in 1956 as a lease property to Naumes Motors Pontiac and Cadillac dealership, eventually becoming Hartman Motors, then Dean Burgers Pontiac, Buick, Cadillac and GMC truck dealership and now Shaheen's Motors, with the same makes.

The author is grateful to Sandra (Howard) Wood for photo and narrative.

223 North Mission Street – Yes, young folks, there really was a person named Col. Harlan Sanders, he lived in Corbin, Kentucky, where he started Kentucky Fried Chicken (or KFC) in his 60s in the early 1960s. In October, 1978, Sanders came to Mt. Pleasant to visit and fry chicken with Mt. Pleasant storeowner Steve Rudoni, who began the local operation in 1976 and whose store won a national award for service in 1978. Sanders visited the Senior Center, attended a banquet in his honor, and visited with Rudoni. In 2010, the KFC continues in the same location.

302 North Mission - The original Pixie Drive-In restaurant was opened by Norm LaBelle at the intersection of Chippewa and Mission streets in 1948 on the corner of the C. F. Turner-Norman LaBelle used car lot. Today's Labelle Management, is owner/operator of restaurants and hotels throughout Michigan, which sprang from that humble beginning.

The orginal Pixie crew posed with owner Norm LaBelle, right, in front of the new eatery to become famous for its unique Coney Island hotdogs. Note Giant Supermarket, another Mt. Pleasant original, in it's second location of the original store, across Mission street to the left .

302 North Mission (continued) - The September, 2006, crew of the Pixie, the cornerstone of the Labelle companies still operating at the same but expanded stand, included, left to right: front row – Dave Scholten - LaBelle Regional Manager, Erica Allen, Dawn Haggart, Teri Cregger, Mallory Esch, Jaime Chellis, Melissa Davis, Matt Trzeciak; second row – Abi Smith, Kristin Sausser, Sara McGuire, Brandi Suder, Drew Cool, Chelsea Binder, Janie Cronstrom, Chris Lagona, Jesse Francek, Amanda Rahkola, Blair Clemmens, Bailey Leasher, Alexia Torres, Sheral Taylor; third row – Brittney Parsons, Amber Phillips, Trisha Winters, Matt Foster, Jamie Jeffers, Michael Formsma, Tim Hadley, Josh Kappa, Shane O'Connor, Kyle Linquist, Patrick Bollinger, Samantha VanHorn, Jen Veit, Perry Cunningham; back row - Stephanie K., Eric Nartken, Jordan Goldner, Jason Horrocks, Casey Bollinger, Erron Sanders, Chris Charnes and Brad Sweet.

The building across the street, peeking from under the roof to the left, was Giant Super Market for many years, then Fortino Food Market, then Gould Rexall Drug Store and in 2010 has been Family Video for more than a decade.

317 North Mission, above, has been one busy building since it's 1949 construction by the fledgling Giant Super Market when that business outgrew its downtown location in the Campbell building. Mt. Pleasant

Mayor I.W. "Bucky" Hartman was on hand when Giant President Les Walton. opened the doors at 317, left. Giant remained in this building until moving to the Campus Mall. In 1964, Fortino's Food Market moved into the building, which was later home to Gould Drug Store, moving in from 502 North Mission.

In 2010, below, the location is occupied by Family Video Rental and Sales.

316 North Mission Street – The small grocery store, above, at the southeast corner of Mission and Lincoln streets was originally Loyd Honewell's "Honey's Hunk and Chunk" meat market and was the first location of Vic's Super Market, now Ric's. At the right is the beginning of construction of the brick building which would house Vic's until the business moved to new quarters at 705 South Mission in the early 1960s. Still on the site in 2010, the building contains: Computers Sales and Service, Cyber's Place, Farmers Insurance Group, Hall of Heros, Shoe Repair, Sports Addix, and Tropical Fish, as well as apartments upstairs. Below, in a not-so-great picture from a 1947 Vic's ad is the staff: Ruth Erler, Ruth Ball, Edna Ervin, Victor Erler (owner), Keith Scott, Woody Allen, Roy Hughes, Rodney Phillips, Lyle Bristol, Carrol Van Ommeren and Albert Clevenger.

319 North Mission was the home of Art Savage Motor Sales in the 1950s, selling first Reos, then Oldsmobiles. Savage eventually left the automobile business, built a sprawling ranch style house at 1005 North Mission Road. Spinning Wheels was built by Roby David Dowling and partner Stephen Lo Cicero at 1241 North Mission Road, on the north corner of Savage's property in Isabella Township north of Mt. Pleasant.

The property became First Automotive in the 1970s and is now St, Germaine's Antiques.

502 North Mission Street - Originally one of the location evolutions of the Fortino Food Market the northeast corner of Crosslanes and Mission Streets was home to Gould Rexall Drugs from the early 1950s, above, until moving to the larger Giant Super Market building, now Family Video, at 317 North Mission in the 1970s. Don Gould later sold Gould Drug Company to Perry Drugs. Meantime, the former Gould site at Mission and Crosslanes streets was occupied by Four Seasons Windows and Siding for about ten years, and has been occupied by Grafx Central commercial printers, below, since the late 1990s.

600 North Mission Street - Built in the 1940s by Fred Gannon, the A & W Drive Inn at the corner of Mission and Andre Streets

served Mt. Pleasant folks frosty root beer mugs and was one of the first of the town's fast food restaurants. Later the location saw Bill and Eva Mourtzouhos, who later owned the Downtown Restaurant, introduced broasted chicken to our menus. More recently, it was Lester's Broasted Chicken, a used book store and in 2010 is home of Central Plumbing, center.

501 North Mission Street– This has been a busy location: Furlong-Bollinger Dodge-Plymouth Sales & Service, above; Campus Chrysler-Plymouth; Leo Beard Lincoln-Mercury; Smith Lincoln-Mercury; and thence finally to Mt. Pleasant Floor Covering, right.

520 North Mission Street - The Texan Restaurant was North Mission Street's most varied-menued sit-down eatery in the 1960s and 1970s. The location is now Central Michigan Urgent Care, a walk-in medical facility.

615-701 North Mission – Look Insurance of Mt. Pleasant at 615 North Mission was once the Rainbow Bar, then Bo-Bo's Bar, then George Heynig's Bar. Look Insurance shares the corner of Mission and Bennett streets on the west side of Mission with Main Street Audio-Video at 701.

701 North Mission – This location was Naumes Motor Sales before that company moved to 116 North Mission, then Loretta's Laundromat for a time, then C & S Yamaha; Rhynard's Tire Service, in the back, and finally Main Street Audio Video, the oldest continuously running video rental business in Mt. Pleasant. Main Street started when Sandy L. Halasz bought Mt. Pleasant Video World, started by Ted Tetreault in 1981. Main Street Audio Video moved to this address in 1991 and expanded into car & home electronics sales and service at that time.

612-616 North Mission Street – Day Electric has been in business at the southeast corner of Mission and Bennett Streets since 1945. Founder George Day grew up in Mt. Pleasant and left to establish a machine shop in Bermuda during World War II, returning to Mt. Pleasant after the war to establish this electrical repair business. Day died in 1989 but the business still operates under the same name, though word "Day", which used to sit atop "Electric", has been removed from the sign. At 616, Dick Switzer operated a barber shop for 42 years, the shop is called Woody's in 2010.

700 North Mission Street - The Scotty Restaurant, above during 1947 curbing and paving of the new US-27 four-lane "super highway" work, was built in 1937. *Continued on the next page*

700 North Mission Street (continued) - Helen and Laurence Warren owned the Scotty Restaurant at this location from 1944 to 1948. Phyllis Stavely Bonstelle claims she made her first hamburger there in 1951 for her uncle. Later the Scotty was owned by Jerry McCord, who went on to built the Avalon Bar east of town. Under McCord's ownership, The Scotty was among Mt. Pleasant's first "open after the bars close" diners. Agnes McDonald bought the building and operated Agnes' Wonderland Diner from 1977 until 2002, above. In 2005, the building was razed to allow for a strip mall, below, anchored by Aaron's Sales.

808 North Mission Street at the southeast corner of Mission and Pickard streets was the site of Fred Phillips original Green Spot Bar, where owner Fred Phillips was on hand to pour a cold one, right.

In 2010, the Green Spot Pub, below, owned for many years by Jerry Sheahan, is thriving under Michael Faulkners ownership. If you want a St. Patrick's Day parking place, you better get it by March 1st.

903 North Mission Street - The 1930-era photo, above looking south at the corner of Pickard and Mission streets, shows some of the Hafer Oil Company employees and the Hafer truck fleet. Standing in front of the building, left to right are: John J. Hafer; Floyd Burgess; Roy D. Hafer; Otis Methner; and Gordon Armstrong. The top floor of Kinney School peeks through the trees behind the building and the billboard on the southwest corner, left middle, occupying the lot where Olson's Tire Company is now located, across Pickard to the south .

Roy D. Hafer and his wife Florence "Flossie" purchased the property in 1926 and built a house there, opening a full-service gasoline filling station on the corner a year later. Hafer Oil Company also delivered gas, fuel oil, kerosene and other petroleum related products to local farmers, homeowners and oil drilling companies in Central Michigan. Their delivery service to oil drilling companies dropped into high gear after the discovery of the Mt. Pleasant oil field east of town on the Isabella/Midland county line, where the Hafers built another filling station at the site of today's Oil City. In the late 1960s, Hafer Oil Company left the gasoline business, leasing the building to the snowmobile dealership of Hafer Hardware next door.

903 North Mission Street (continued) - In 1981, the gas station site was sold, the station and house demolished and the Flap Jack Restaurant was built there, later to become Filmore's Restaurant until demolition in 2008. Just north of the corner on the west side of Mission Street, a full sevice hardware was started in 1947 by John J. Hafer and his stepfather Gordon Jones. In 1950, John D. Hafer took over the entire building and expanded the hardware business in addition to becoming a large Ski Doo brand snowmobile dealer. John Hafer retired in 1983, selling the business, which retained the Hafer name until closing in 2008, to Glen Irwin. Mt. Pleasant's second Walgreen's location, below, opened on the site in 2009.

CHAPTER 5: EAST SIDE

415 East Chippewa Street is on the northwest corner of Chippewa Street and Fancher Avenue. John D. Doughty, a printer by trade, had come to Mt. Pleasant in 1872 to take over publication of one of the village's newspapers, *The Enterprise*, which he bought upon the death of its owner, Albert Fox. Somewhere in the course of life he met Eva Craig Graves, of Warsaw, Kentucky.

In 1873, he promised to build her "the most beautiful home in town" as an inducement to come to Mt. Pleasant . This is the house they built and they were married May 24, 1874.

In 1875 the printing office and all its fixtures were destroyed by fire. There was no insurance. Doughty ordered a new press from Detroit and set up office in the parlor of his home, issuing the next issue of *The Enterprise* on its regular day the following week. The newspaper was printed from here until new offices were built. The marks on the floor made by the printing press have been preserved by each owner of the house since.

John and Eva edited the newspaper together and she, being a devout suffrage worker, brought Susan B,. Anthony to town and was her hosts when she came to lecture on the suffrage cause. The sherrif locked them out of the courthouse and Anthony gave her lecture at Carr & Grangers's Hall downtown on March 17, 1879.

John Doughty owned *The Enterprise* until 1885, when he sold to A. S. Conant to pursue other business interests until his 1907 death.

For more than 40 years, the 1920s to 1960s, the house was owned by the Charles Wildermuth, an oil man, and family. After Charles death, Mrs. Wildermuth managed to make her money last, selling the back portion of the property in the 1940s, where a house was built, see 315 North Fancher in Chapter 3. Later owners included Jack and Cora Neyer, who bought the house in 1998 and sold it in 2000. The house remains, in 2010, well maintained and orderly.

201 East Pickard Street, above, was the site of a plant operating from the late 1910s to late 1930s to process the chicory abundant in mid-Michigan. Chicory is a homeopathic medicine sometimes used as a coffee substitute.The plant closed in the 1930s.

In 2010, below, the site is the home of the ReStore, managed by George Sponseller, which accepts donations of all sorts of merchandise and building materials, resold to the public to benefit Habitat for Humanity.

4833 Crosslanes Street, Mary McGuire Elementary School – Mary McGuire began teaching at 17 years old in 1902 at a small country school in Isabella County's Chippewa Township with a limited bachelor's degree with limited certificate from Central Michigan Normal School and ultimately received her Masters Degree from Columbia University in New York. She taught at Chippewa, Longwood and Broomfield schools. Her first teaching job in Mt. Pleasant was at the West Side School, later Ganiard. She taught in Mt. Pleasant schools for 15 years before becoming an elementary school principal of the Maple Street Fancher School and Kinney School. The Mary McGuire School was dedicated in her honor in the early 1960s. Although nearly 50 years old, Mary McGuire School is the newest in the Mt. Pleasant School system, built in a timeless style so the old pictures of the entrance look amazingly like the new pictures. The original building has been expanded over the years. She died in 1969. In the 2009-2010 School Year, Mary McGuire had enrolled approximately 194 students, 90 fifth graders and 104 sixth graders, with a teaching staff totaling 13 teachers.

105 East High Street - The High Street Apartments, owned by
Patrick Hayden, opened in 1933, above, with first-year residents
listed as Emmett Caltrider, Harry Wilson, Jess Crontz and Blanche
Scott. The building was formerly a hospital from the turn of the
20th Century until the 1920s. First housing newcomers during the
Mt. Pleasant Field oil boom, the building has undergone a number
of changes in appearance, below, and the nature of its tenancy,
with later city directory listings seeming to indicate some CMU
student's occupancy.

301 East High Street - Charles Grawn, builder of this house at the northeast corner of High and Franklin streets was from Salem, Michigan. He came to Mt. Pleasant in 1899 and was appointed president, of Central Michigan Normal School and Business Institute in 1890. During his 1890-1918 tenure, the training school, power plant, gymnasium and science building were built and the campus grew to 25 acres. Charles Grawn Hall opened in 1915 and is the oldest building on campus. Later the address was home to Central President Dr. Eugene Charles Warriner. Below, in 2010, note the balcony has been retained over the front door and the latticework on the windows remains.

425 East Broadway Street – The General Agency was founded in 1915 upstairs over a storefront at 129 East Broadway by three Isabella County pioneer stock; Charles A. Carnahan, Walter W. Russell and Glen C. Riley. Carnahan's son Clifford "Cliff" Carnahan joined the firm in 1938 and Tip's son-in-law Jack Weisenburger joined the organization in 1954. In 1977, Jack's son Bob, now president of the company, joined the firm. In 2010 General Agency is one of the oldest continuous businesses in Mt. Pleasant and is one of the state's largest insurance agencies.

Across Kinney Boulevard from General Agency, but at 104 North Kinney is American Cleaners, begun at 219 South Main Street in the 1940s in 2010 still in the Knight family.

706 East Broadway Street – An eight page supplement to the *Isabella County Times* announced the opening of the J. F. Battle ultra-modern automobile dealership April 7, 1938, Battle continued business until the 1960s, when George Smale bought the Chevrolet Dealership. Later it became Archey Brothers Sales and Service until the 1990s when the building became the business home of Kinney Wholesale, operating from there in 2010.

705 East Broadway Street – This was the third and final Mt. Pleasant home for the Atlantic and Pacific Tea Company, A & P company store in the late 1960s. When A & P closed its Mt. Pleasant operation, former employee Don Steebey and Marguerite Rice went into the grocery business here as D & M Foodland until the late 1980s. In 2010, it is Bringham's NAPA Auto Parts of Mt. Pleasant.

1017 East Broadway Street – Grandmother Mary Morse poses in front of her home with Mary Neebes and Claribel Neebes. The long shed built on the house at the right was used to store wood and coal as well as the vegetables the family raised and sold to augment their income. According to Mary Morse's granddaughter Janet Holman of Mt. Pleasant, the fence was to keep the sheep and cattle that were regularly herded past the house out of the family's garden. Later the dust and noise of Broadway Street, earlier called just "the road to Saginaw", got to be too much and the Morses moved to Wisconsin Street in Mt. Pleasant. Below, in 2010 the house is part of the Broadway Apartments property.

600 Block of East Pickard Street, north side – In 1947, above, the brand new Mt. Pleasant Municipal Water Tower reigns 139 feet over the empty field in the above photo taken probably from the present Olson Tire Service location. That's the old Crystal Ice Company ice plant, where ice was manufactured and stored, in the lower left. Below, the same scene in 2010, showing the western edge of the Walgreen's North parking lot at the right and Mr. Muffler below the tower. The old ice house is not visible because of the trees but is still there, now used for storage by Rise Machine Company.

704 East Pickard Street – In 1959, John Olson started a tire business with one bay and a gasoline filling pump behind a coin laundry at 701 North Mission. He was managing the business for Lyle Rhynard in Shepherd. In 1960, John bought the business from Rhynard and opened as Olson Tire Service at its present location, adding bays and adding to the cinderblock building, shown above in 2004 and below in 2010.

Business grew, and when a convenience store to the east at the corner of Pickard and Mission went out of business, Olson acquired that lot for overflow parking and annually displays a nativity scene at that busy intersection at Christmas time, to the delight of local Christians. Sons Tim and Pat Olson bought the business from their dad in 1998 and continue to operate the business, with an eye to someday having it pass to the hands of Tim's son Joshua.

Two East Pickard businesses with business roots elsewhere – Krapohl Ford Lincoln Mercury, above, started in 1950 when Harold and Bob Krapohl left their respective jobs at Firestone Tire and a car dealership in Grand Rapids to resurrect a defunct Ford dealership at 114 Court Street in Mt. Pleasant, inset. In 1970, in need of more room, they moved the business to 1415 East Pickard. Bob and Harold retired in 1975, with management passing to Bob's son-in-law Brian Smith and Harold's son Tom Krapohl, who added the Lincoln and Mercury car lines in 1981. The dealership remains in the family in 2010.

Wendel's Home Furnishings in 2010 at 5260 East Pickard, above, has been in this location for two years, having begun in 1980 at 1015 North Mission, then spending over 20 years at 900 North Mission, the present Advance Auto Parts location.

4650 East Pickard, Street the site of today's Heritage AutoMall, was the location of a World War II prisoner of war camp for captured German soldiers. Prisoners worked on area farms, roads, and other projects. Many former prisoners remember their stay at Mt. Pleasant fondly because of their humane treatment here.

1019 East Broadway Street – In the early 1930s Tom Milloy, grandfather of Tom and John Olson, built a stylized wide-body airplane replica in his field behind his Broadway Apartments complex here, using parts of two train cars, but no airplane parts, and fabricating the "wings". The "plane" was moved to the corner of Mission and Valley roads north of Mt. Pleasant, where it was a popular all-night diner, owned by Bernie Cusbert, until wind blew off one of the "wings" in the early 1950s and the diner never re-opened.

CHAPTER 6: SOUTH END

302 South Fancher Street was the home of Lewis N. Marsh of Marsh & Lewis, a mercantile store established in 1879 at the northeast corner of Main and Broadway that the partners purchased in 1889 from founder Frank M. Foster. L. N. Marsh died in 1927. In 1948, the house was occupied by C. F. Knollenberg and in 1976 by George B. Martin.
In 2010, the house is a rental with two apartments and continues to keep its gracious appearance.

302 South Fancher Street – On this Mt. Pleasant site in 1882, an eight room Union School, a high school was built for a cost of $15,000. Above, students, parents, and townspeople turned out in pride at the opening, making education beyond the eight grades of rural schools readily available to the area's youth. By 1908, a "twin" addition to the Union School had been built to the south. The school had ten teachers and a 1,500 book library.

302 South Fancher (continued) – By 1928, the cupolas had been stripped from the high school and eighth grade added in 1908. This building served as a high school until 1957 and as a junior high school until the late 1960s when age and deterioration forced its abandonment and demolition. In 1969, Illinois Street was vacated and Sacred Heart Catholic Church with rectory was built at the old high school location.

701 South University Street – The turreted house, above, was built around 1901 by building contractor Lewis D. Cole of Cole Brothers contracting. The Cole brothers built many of the buildings at the Mt. Pleasant Indian Industrial Schools, the Mt. Pleasant Library.

His home was a showcase of his skill, which has stood the test of time, as witnessed by the 2010 photo at the right.

702 South University – Howard E. Chatterton built on the corner where Normal meets Cherry Street, above. Howard, the son in Chatterton & Son, a company that started out as grocers in 1900, then bought the Horning elevator at the northwest corner of Main and Lincoln and became the town's most extensive handlers of grain, hay, wool, potatoes and apples. He was a graduate of Michigan Agricultural College and Central Michigan Normal College. H. E. Chatterton was in the grocery business in Bowling Green, Ohio, and purchasing agent for a wholesale house in Toledo, Ohio, before returning to Mt. Pleasant. The house, was the home of Mrs. T. U. Fuller in the 1940s, and was Beacon House, an Isabella County home for wayward children until the county disposed of it in 1976. In 2010, it is a private residence.

704 South University– Rising three stories above its two story neighbors, this home was built by Fred F. L. Keeler, for his mother, wife and two children. Keeler was appointed to the Central Michigan Normal School faculty in 1895 as an instructor and head of the Department of Science. In 1908, two years after the above photo was taken, Keeler left Central to become Deputy Superintendent of Public Instruction at Lansing. In 1913, he was appointed Michigan Superintendent of Public Instruction and was elected to that position until his death at 46 years old. Keeler Union, now Powers Hall, on the Central campus, where separate floors provided lounges and game rooms for men and women, was named for Professor Keeler in 1939.

For several years it was the home of Ray F. Cline, local business- man and founder of Ray F. Cline Advertising and Clinemark at 209 West Broadway. In 2010, it continues as a private residence.

711 South Fancher Street – Alexander Hall, a boot and shoemaker from Montgomery County, New York, came to the Mt. Pleasant area in 1874 and opened a shop. In 1877, he bought 40 acres of land in Section 15, Union Township, Isabella County, adjacent to the town, which, after platting 20 acres, he annexed to the town in 1878. Hall retained a five acre wooded plot for himself, in the middle of which he built a house. Hall's house burned in 1913 and his widow sold the property to William E. Harris of Harris Mill, who built the imposing brick mansion, above,. The Edward O. Harris family sold the property and home to J. Walter Leonard of Leonard Refineries in the 1950s. The Leonards lived in the house for many years before selling to a prominent local sand and gravel company chain owner in the 1970s. In 2010, the huge wooded lot is immaculately landscaped and, owing to its location at the northeast corner of Fancher at High Street, also West M-20, is a prominent landmark for motorists coming to or passing through Mt. Pleasant.

900 South Main Street – Noted Mt. Pleasant builder William A. McRae came here in 1892 from his native Ontario, Canada, bringing almost twenty years of building trades experience with him, which he immediately put to work in the thriving Mt. Pleasant market for residential building. He also brought his large family of seven children, all of whom he insisted attend Central Normal School, just a few blocks down Main Street. In 2010, porch gone, the home is a Fraternity house for students of McRae's beloved Central Michigan, now University.

514 South Main Street - Built in 1895 by prominent Mt. Pleasant attorney Michael Devereaux, the turreted and gingerbreaded house became the second Mt. Pleasant home for Dr. Albert T. and Ella Getchell, see previous page, following Devereaux's 1911 death. By this time Dr. Getchell was in his mid-60s and the front room of this house afforded him a smaller space to continue his limited practice until his 1933 death. Dr. Getchell was a member of the Mt. Pleasant Knights of Pythias, who presided over ceremonies at

the laying of the cornerstone of Central Michigan Normal School's first administration building in September, 1892. Above right, in 2010, the address is home to the Phi Sigma Sigma Sorority.

601 South Main Street – Built in 1904 by lumber/banking magnate John S. Weidman, this was his residence until his 1919 death. John S. Weidman was born in Lenockee Township of St. Clair County, Michigan in 1852, one of twelve children. The family resided there until 1866, when they moved to Mecosta County just south of Big Rapids. He began his working life as a river log driver at age 16. Weidman rose rapidly in the lumber business world. He married Margaret A. Mitchell at Big Rapids and they raised six children. In 1903, Weidman bought a private bank in Mt. Pleasant and incorporated the Isabella County State Bank. For a time in the 1940s, the house was the offices of Sohio oil and gas company. In 2010, the address is home to Zeta Alpha Fraternity.

251 South Brown Street, Pullen Elementary School, shown above in 1955, was named for Dr. Charles D. Pullen, a prominent Mt. Pleasant surgeon, physician and civic leader. Born in 1884 at Allegan, Michigan, Dr. Pullen came to Mt. Pleasant following graduation with a Medical Degree from University of Michigan in 1892. He continued honing his professional skills with post-graduate courses in Chicago and New York, while expanding his Mt. Pleasant practice. He was physician for the Mt. Pleasant Indian Industrial Schools for ten years, serving on the Mt. Pleasant Board of Education for five years and was a captain in the U.S. Army during World War I. About Dr. Pullen, Isaac A. Fancher in his 1911 *Past and Present of Isabella County*, said "Aside from his profession, he is interested in whatever makes for the material prosperity of his city and county, takes an active part in all measures for the general welfare of his fellow men and meets his every responsibility as one who knows his duty and, 'knowing. dares maintain'." He was elected to the 1935 Michigan Legislature.

Dr. Pullen died in 1940 and the school named for him was erected in the early 1950s. In the 2009-2010 school year, Pullen School enrolled approximately 86 kindergarteners, 72 first graders, 76 second graders, 61 third graders and 60 fourth graders for a total of about 355 students, taught by 18 teachers.

I attended the 1st year it opened.
3rd - 7th grade

314 South Brown Street – The Davis Clinic, a forerunner of today's multi-doctor private clinics, was an association of doctors who pooled resources and equipment assets more economically maintaining individual offices. The clinic was built on South Brown Street in 1952 by Fred Gannon, whose working notes appear in the lower left of the above photograph. For many years, the clinic, shown below in a 1989 newspaper advertising photograph, was very popular. Gradually, the founding doctors retired or expired and the influx of younger new doctors faded to a trickle. The Davis Clinic closed in the 1990s. In 2010, the building is occupied by the offices of a variety of medical specialists including: Asthma & Allergy, Dr. Atchoo DO, Dr. James Caldwell MD, Miracle Ear, Mt. Pleasant Medical Practice, and Sunrise Physical Therapy.

801 South Kinney Street, Fancher Elementary School – One of Mt. Pleasant's most unique conundrums is that the school named for one of Mt. Pleasant's most prominent pioneers, Isaac A. Fancher, has never

been located on the street also named for him. The first Fancher School, left, was located at 309 West Maple Street in the late 1800s and was known as the "Maple Street Fancher School".

Fancher's life and accomplishments are dealt with in great detail in Chapter 2 in the section addressing North Main Street.

In 1936, the base structure of the school was built occupying almost all of the 800 block facing South Kinney Street and all the block except the lots lining Mission Street to the east, above. In 2009-2010 school year 152 fifth graders and 150 sixth graders were enrolled at Fancher for a total of 302 students, with 21 teachers.

we lived just two doors down from this building on College

1088-1099 South University – Originally the campus supply store here was called Zwergels. N. G. Gover, recognized the business opportunity available by offering goods to the students stranded on the "remote" Central campus, and bought grocery and school supply store at the south terminus of Normal at Bellows streets in the early 1900s, left inset. A sporting goods store, beauty shop bookstore and restaurant added to the Gover enterprise and by the late 1940s, right inset, the building on University atBellows Streets was anchored by Cole's Central Supply Company. Cole's later added on to the back of the building and moved into that wing, putting the University Shop, a clothing store, on the corner, with Archey's Sporting Goods and Jack's Campus Grill filling the south section of the building facing College Street, above.

The entire structure burnt to the ground April 7,1963, killing three Central Michigan University students when a cornice fell: Cheerie Lou Anderson, a 20 year old sophomore from Cheboygan; Robert Powers, a 20 year old sophomore from Marshall; and Matthew Tachywooge, an exchange student from Bankok Thialand. Additionally, Mt. Pleasant volunteer fireman Leo Edward Ream, 49 year old manager of Northwood Dairy, had a heart attack and died fighting the blaze.

1088-1099 South University (continued) –Following the devastating 1963 fire, the University Plaza shopping complex was rebuilt, containing the Student Book Exchange supply store, below, the shopping center and its former tenant, now neighbor the Malt Shop, remains a favorite student venue. The Malt Shop was later built across the street at 1088 South University. The complex is shown below in a 2006 winter picture.

1560 South Watson Street, Vowles Elementary School was named for Hannah M. Vowles, who was born Hannah Mary Shorts in Canada in 1869. Graduating high school at Traverse City, Michigan, in June, 1887, she came to Mt. Pleasant the following September to teach at the Crowley School, located about where the Target store is on Bluegrass Road in 2010. She taught in the Mt. Pleasant school system from 1888 to 1898. She married Charles E. Vowles here in 1898 and taught college Sunday School at the First Methodist Church for twenty-five years.

Hannah M. Vowles was the first woman to be elected to public office in Mt. Pleasant when she was elected to the Board of Education in July, 1917, where she served as Secretary to the Board. She was active in the Mt. Pleasant Women's Club, served as president, and was vice president of the Michigan Federation of Women's Clubs. She lived to see Vowles School named for her in the late 1950 and often expressed that the honor was the high point of her life. She died in 1963.

During the 2009-2010 school year, 100 kindergarteners, 86 first graders, 89 second graders, 73 third graders and 71 fourth graders were enrolled at Vowles for a total of 419 students, taught by 21 teachers.

1155 South Elizabeth Street, Mt. Pleasant High School (MPHS) – In 1956, after several attempts by the Board of Education for a new high school, voters consented and construction began. Just before the school opened in the fall of 1957, Mt. Pleasant High School 1957-1958 Student Council President-elect Larry Stinson toured the new facility with Mt. Pleasant Superintendent of School Russell LeCronier, third from left, and visiting dignitaries interested in the school courtyard architecture.

In the 2009-2010 school year MPHS enrolled approximately 1200 students in grades 9-12, with 42 teachers. The school, below in 2010, has state of the art facilities including an 800 seat auditorium and 2,800 seat gymnasium. New facilities, including the Area Technical Center, offer students an optimal environment and a wide variety of educational opportunities. The school expresses pride in their diverse academic curriculums, experienced teaching staff, and students.

CHAPTER 7: CENTRAL MICHIGAN UNIVERSITY

According to the Wikipedia online dictionary –"A **normal school** was a school created to train high school graduates to be teachers. Its purpose was to establish teaching standards or *norms*, hence its name. Most such schools are now called **teachers' colleges**; however, in some places, the term *normal school* is still used."

How a normal school at Mt. Pleasant named Central came to be, and its evolution into today's Central Michigan University is the tale of the single-minded, tireless efforts of one man - Samuel W. Hopkins. A Mt. Pleasant attorney and realtor, Hopkins was the godfather of the seedling institution destined to be the fourth largest university in Michigan. You'll get a chance to get better acquainted with Mr. Hopkins later in this chapter. Meantime, let's discuss how Central was born.

In the late 1800s, the teachers of Isabella County each year held a Teachers Institute at the county seat in Mt. Pleasant. During these institutes, tests would be given to high school graduates who wanted to become school teachers. If the person passed the tests, they were awarded a Teacher's Certificate. The number of one-room rural schools in the county *(ultimately to reach 115)* was growing and the demand for teachers was intense. Yet in 1882, the week-long summer institute was sparsely attended.

By 1890, there were an estimated 4,500 students who regularly attended classes an average seven months per year, according to *The Enterprise* newspaper. These students were taught by 136 teachers, of which only three had teacher's certificates.

1892, the month-long summer normal had only 45 enrollees. The failure rate was so high that it was determined that the establishment of a bonafide normal school was needed. The year before only 10 out of 58 passed the teachers test.

M. K. Skinner, who had bought H. W. Jordan's Pen Art and Business College in 1891 planned to make improvements and add a full normal course, so people who wish to be teachers to earn a teachers certificate.

Samuel Hopkins, knowing 60 acres of the old Hursh farm at the south city limits were available, sketched a proposed sub-division, believing the sale of lots would make enough money to finance erection of a normal school building. He approached others with his plan.

Central's first home. – On September 13, 1892, the Central Michigan Normal School and Business Institute opened its doors on the second floor of the Carpenter Building at the southeast corner of Main and Michigan Streets, shown above in the 1970s, upstairs over the Mt. Pleasant, later Smith's Drug Store. Michigan Historical Marker # L69C, was installed in 1968 at second floor level on the north side of the building facing Michigan Street reading: "Founded in 1892 as a private institution, Central Michigan Normal School and Business Institute held its first classes on this site. The institution became a state normal school in 1895. After several changes in name, the school became Central Michigan University."

The building burned in the late 1990s, but the historical marker was saved and in 2010 resides on the CMU campus alongside the Peace Pond on East Campus Drive near Mission Street.

At September 18, 1892, ceremonies the Central Michigan Normal School and Business Institute, officially broke ground for the school's first building on a ten acre plot south of town. On November 19, 1892, the cornerstone of the first building was laid in ceremonies conducted by the Knights of Pythias.

With this vision fresh in his mind, Hopkins talked it over with friend, farmer and fellow member of the board of education Charles Brooks, who reacted favorably. The two shared the idea with John W. Hance, Michael Devereaux and A. S. Conant. That five then invited Wilkinson Doughty, George Dusenbury, Isaac A. Fancher, M. Lower, Douglas Nelson, F. D. Patterson, and L. N. Smith, to serve on a planning committee with them. The twelve formed the Mount Pleasant Improvement Company with a capital of $10,000 in shares of $25, which bought the 60 Hursh acres. Eight acres had already been subdivided, so company land consisted of 52 acres, with ten acres set aside for the college campus. The company sold 151 housing lots at a July 4, 1892 auction, for $110 each with the buyer asked to place $10 down and pay $10 per month for the second and third months and $5 per month on the balance until paid.

In private hands until 1895, Central Michigan Normal School and Business Institute became Central Michigan Normal School, a state institution, that year. The main administration building was augmented by a wing addition to the west in 1899, with another added to the west in 1902 to meet growing space needs of the robust young school.

Old Main was a great venue and backdrop for events and businesses, with Normal Street running right to the front door, above. Center, the 1903 Mt. Pleasant fire department posed there, as did Montgomery Bus Lines of Mt. Pleasant, bottom.

The campus expanded from ten to twenty-five acres in 1894 to encompass an area from Hopkins to Preston between Main and Franklin Streets. To provide a place for prospective teachers to gain classroom experience face to face with actual students, the Central Training School was built.

Central Hall was opened in 1909 as the first gymnasium on campus. World War I soldiers trained in the building, as did World War Two naval officers. Following 1951 completion of Finch Fieldhouse, the Central Hall Physical Sciences Building became the Reserve Officer Training (R.O.T.C.) building until late 1970s demolition to leave a foundation" footprint near a new

library building, presently the "new" Ronan Hall, and southern expansion of Grawn Hall. The postcard on which the view above appears reads "Girls in Training, Central Normal School Gym."

Charles Grawn Hall, above, on the west side of the Central core campus mall, opened in 1915 as the Science and Agricultural Building, survived two fires *(in 1933 and again in 1954)* to become the oldest building on campus. Upon opening, the building contained the Agriculture, Psychology, Biology, Physics and Chemistry departments and housed the university print shop for a time. In 1965, following addition of a south wing, Grawn Hall became home to the Business Department. The Applied Business Studies Complex, in a north wing of Grawn Hall, was added in 1989 on a site once occupied by a greenhouse attached to the science building. The Applied Business Studies Complex, partially funded by a $400,000 Dow Chemical Company donation, is home to the LaBelle Entrepreneurial Center, named for Mount Pleasant restaurateur Norman LaBelle.

The Central State Normal School football squad of 1912 poses at the edge of the athletic field behind Old Central Hall on the west side of the campus mall, approximately where Wightman Hall, on Washington Street now stands. In the background is the smokestack of the first campus power plant. While there are more people in the photo than the 1912 football team roster in the 1913 Central yearbook, those named, who played for Coaches Bruce Strickland and Harry Helmer are: Gerald Stilwell – Captain; Floyd Smith – Right Tackle; Leo Going – Left Tackle; Grover A. Buchan – Left Guard; Francis Campbell – Right Guard,; Ray Cheney – Left End; Frank Davidson – Left End; Ray Watkins – Left Halfback; Allen Graham – Right End; Dave Davidson – Left Tackle; Archie Leonard – Right Halfback; Russell Fraser – Fullback; and Marcel Lafromboise – Right End.

By the early 1930s, the cupola on the Training School had disappeared, as had the flanking peaks and two smaller chimneys. Roof dormers had been added, apparently as a nod to more modern heating systems.

Two devastating fires in less than a decade changed the face of Central's campus forever. On December 7, 1925, Central lost its main office and 30,000 volume library, above.

Temporary buildings were quickly erected and work began immediately on Warriner Hall. The next victim of conflagration was the Training School on January 10, 1933. Bricks from the building were used to create the track around the new alumni field on the east side of campus.

Providing new administration offices, an auditorium and a library for the burgeoning Central State Teachers College, Warriner Hall, above, at completion, note lack of trees, was named for College President Eugene E. Warriner, and dedicated June 17, 1928, replacing "Old Main", the school's first building. Warriner Hall, remains the most enduring symbol of "Central".

The building that's had the most names of any on campus. The College Elementary School (updated name for the Training School) was built on the east side of the core campus mall, where the original Training School was destroyed by fire in 1933. The current Woodward C. Smith Hall was North Hall, housing the Business Administration Department after the 1958 Elementary School moved to Rowe Hall. The building became Woodward Smith Hall in 1984 and houses the Management and Law and Marketing Department and Hospitality Services Administration Department.

The Log Alumni Museum. - Once nestled in the woodlands of the eastern portion of the Central Michigan College campus, an 1800s hand-hewn log cabin known as the Central Alumni Museum, nestled in the forest facing Franklin Street, location 1 in the photograph below, on property owned by the Central Alumni Association. The cabin,

purchased in 1923 from Deerfield Township farmer Charles McCarthy, was outfitted by CMU former Dean of Women Bertha Ronan in a  pioneer theme and housed artifacts typical of the frontier family's abode. The "Alumni Association Land" east of Franklin street was purchased by Central and was site of the first Alumni Field, below, the original location of the Central Alumni Museum. For many years the cabin served as a meeting place for alumni groups, college organizations and local Boy Scout and Girl Scout organizations. In 1949, plans were made for a state of the art fieldhouse to be located near the corner of Franklin Street and Preston Street, then all residential on the south side.

"$150 cabin to make room for $1,000,000 fieldhouse" proclaimed a 1950 Mt. Pleasant *Daily Times-News* headline. Finch Fieldhouse was built and

 the Alumni Museum log cabin and contents were moved across the street to the college woods behind Warriner Hall, location 2 in the photo on the left.

.In 1959, the cabin was dismantled to make room for the new University Center and the woods disappeared, along with the artifacts contained therein, apparently.

The exact occasion isn't known but the people at this graduation event are, left to right: front - CMU President Judson Foust, Dwight Rich, Dr. Susan B. Riley, Frank Hartman and Virgil Rolland.. Back- Col. Fossum, Woody Smith, Carlo Barberi, Dr. Moore, Father Goodrow, Dean Sorrels, and Dean Rickmeyer.

This Photograph of Central faculty emeritus and spouses is believed to have been taken around 1965 and includes, left to right: front – Ethel Pirroat, Myrtle Maybee, Rollie Mayhew, Claude Love, Geneva Love, Gerritt Muyskens, Mae Beck, and Earl Beck. Back – Ivan Cole, Frances Cole, Charles Anspach, Mary Anspach, Dr. Kenneth Barber, Margaret Depuy, George Depuy, Ella O'Neil, Dean Louise Sharp, and Helen Johnson.

At the dedication of Warriner Hall June 17, 1928, named for Central State Teachers College President (1918-1939) Eugene E. Warriner, President Warriner predicted: "While we have made many changes in the past few years, we feel we have only begun to develop and to grow." Comparison of the campus 1910 on the sixth page of this chapter with this current Central Michigan University campus map seems to fulfill Warriner's vision, along with that of the unsung thousands who have along the way made the University of 2010 a springboard to an expanded future. This progress has come about through the generosity of time and financial support by generations of students, faculty and alumni along with the general community.

In 2010, Central Michigan University with a total enrollment of 27,500 (20,000 undergraduate and 7,500 graduate students), is currently the state's fourth largest. The university offers its growing student population a broad selection of more than 3,000 individual courses and a choice of 29 degrees.

Nearly 20,500 students live on the 480 acre campus in Central Michigan University's 6,441 student rooms housed at 22 residence halls. There are 823 full-time CMU faculty members and more than 160,000 alumni. In addition, the University has 41 off-campus centers of learning.

IN MEMORY OF AGNES CAMPBELL

From a February, 1955, edition of Central Life,
Central Michigan Teachers College, Mt. Pleasant, Michigan
By Franklin K. Killian, Associate Professor, Rural Education

NOTE: The author is grateful to Lucille (Konyha) Hrivnak of Trenton, Michigan, for sharing this article, which reflects the dedication of the "teachers who teach teachers" at Central Michigan College. "It was my good fortune" Hrivnak said in the note accompanying this article "to have her help build the foundation for my teaching career, which lasted 34 years"

On the last day of January, 1955, Central lost one of its beloved instructors in the rural laboratory schools. Mrs. Campbell began teaching in the college laboratory schools in 1942. She brought to this position, years of rich varied experiences and training. She imbued in her students, as few teachers are empowered, a love of the teaching profession.

Agnes Hanson Campbell was born in Copenhagen, Denmark, February 7, 1892. Her father trained in engineering, was an officer in the Danish army. Agnes, at the age of eight, with her father and mother immigrated to America. The family settled at Grayling where her father was employed with Hanson and Sons for thirty-three years. Agnes Hanson was married to Willard Campbell of Mount Pleasant, June 17, 1916.

Mrs. Campbell was bilingual since she received training in the Danish Elementary Schools and the American High Schools and Colleges. The first professional training which Mrs. Campbell received was at Central. She was graduated from the elementary program in 1912. She taught in Mount Pleasant schools from 1912 to 1915. She did substitute teaching in Central's training school. Since she was an accomplished musician, she taught violin for five years under J. H. Powers, director of music, at this college.

The Bachelor of Arts degree was granted to her by Central Michigan College and the Master of Arts degree by the University of Michigan. She did graduate work at the University of Chicago, University of Maine, and George Peabody College of Education.

The trust and warm affection given her by little children was a measure of the quality of her teaching. Her companionship was sought by a host of friends whose lives she has benefited in one way or another.

She was intimate with living growing things. Her school with a rural environment became a laboratory. She encouraged young minds to explore in a dynamic world of action, color, and distance. She loved the good earth. To her science was more fascinating than literature.

Little time was available for leisure in Mrs. Campbell's busy life. With her husband, she did, however, take time to drive slowly along country roads, where she could observe trees, flowers, animals and birds. A walk in the woods was an inspiration.

Among her hobbies was the collection of bird and animal specimens common to Michigan. The collections were authorized by special permits from the Federal and State governments. The specimens were often gifts from the Department of Conservation or friends. Sometimes she found the specimens along the highways where automobiles had taken their toll. She never killed.

Mrs. Campbell was well-known throughout Michigan and many states of the union where her exhibits of science materials and integrated art thrilled her audiences. Her appreciation of nature, science, art, and music was so definitely a part of her life pattern that she easily influenced others toward her beliefs. Her life's timeless qualities will continue to mold boys and girls through the teaching of more than a hundred fifty people she helped to train in the laboratory schools. Here was a

In the spring of 1951, teacher Agnes H. Campbell, right, who taught in Central's rural laboratory schools from 1942 through 1954, joined at Hoag School by Miss Lucille Koyha on the left and Miss Fowler in the middle, student teachers from Central Michigan College of Education.

master teacher... one, who could stand to be counted for wholesome personality, kind disposition, and Christian character.

Samuel Whaley Hopkins
April 1, 1845 – August 29, 1923

Central Michigan University owes its existence to one man, who fought to bring an institution devoted to teaching teachers to Mt. Pleasant, persuading reluctant investors to form the Mt. Pleasant Improvement Company and later taking his cause to the Michigan Senate to win state accreditation for the school that organization founded. But for him, Central might not have existed and the face of Mt. Pleasant would be forever changed.

Samuel Hopkins, below in 1906, was born April 1, 1845, to cotton manufacturer Samuel Hopkins and Freelove Burlingame Hopkins in Exeter, Rhode Island. One of his ancestors was Judge Edward Whalley, who fled England under the rule of Charles II. To distinguish himself from his father so there would not be two Samuel Hopkins abroad, young Samuel adopted the middle name Whaley (one "l") early in life. Samuel W. was the youngest of the Hopkins nine children.

After graduating from Bryant & Stratton Business College of Cleveland, Ohio, in 1865, he spent a few years selling books and teaching before entering the Law Department of the Michigan University, where he graduated in 1872. He moved to Grand Rapids, Michigan, where he was

admitted to the Michigan Bar. While in Clare, Michigan Hopkins met the honorable Isaac A. Fancher, who persuaded him to move to the booming village of Mt. Pleasant and to become a partner in Fancher's law firm. The two practiced law together for three years. Bad health forced Hopkins through a number of law partnerships until in 1873, he joined with Daniel E. Lyon in the real-estate, insurance and loan business. Ten years later, they represented eleven insurance companies and were the largest business in that line in Isabella County.

176

His keen interest in politics saw him appointed Union Township Clerk in 1873 and elected to that position for three consecutive terms. He then served seven years as Justice of the Peace and two years as deputy township clerk while serving as justice. He was superintendent of schools for Union Township at Mt. Pleasant, and was Mt. Pleasant Superintendent of Schools, along with being a member of the board of education for Mt. Pleasant. He was Mt. Pleasant's first village attorney.

In 1874, he platted the Hopkins Addition to Mt. Pleasant, bounded: on the north by a line of two lots south East Maple Street from the alley between South Lansing and South Main Streets; on the south one block on High Streets and a block and a half from South University the alleyway between South Lansing and South Franklin streets; on the east by four lots facing south Franklin Street and South University from East Cherry Street to High Street; and on the west by a line of two lots south of Maple Street to High Street. He also, with law partner Daniel Lyon, platted the Hopkins-Lyon Addition to Mt. Pleasant, bounded: on the north by Fessenden Street; on the south by Upton Avenue; on the east by Harris Street and on the west by South Henry Street, west of the Chippewa River.

In 1875-1876, Hopkins was Isabella County Prosecuting Attorney and his chief claim to fame during that tenure was reforming the northeastern Isabella County village of Loomis, a wild and wooly lumber camp town. In 1877-1880, he was elected and served as a representative of the Isabella District in the Michigan House of Representatives.

1892 was a busy year for Hopkins. As Chairman of the Mt. Pleasant Business Men's Association, he had charge of the work of  locating the United States Indian Schools in Isabella County, corresponding with authorities in Washington and with Congressman Bliss, representative from the Mt. pleasant area, see Chapter 11 on the Indian Schools.

 Also in 1892, he conceived the idea for the erection of the normal school, see start of this chapter.

In 1892, he was elected to the Michigan Senate and waged a campaign to get Central state-accredited, which he accomplished in 1895, a year after leaving Senate service.

After 1900, he took very little interest in politics, having been defeated in 1898 in a bid for national office. For several more years Hopkins continued to promote the Mt. Pleasant area, serving as president of the Mt. Pleasant Sugar Company.

The Michigan Condensed Milk Factory (Borden Creamery) in Mt. Pleasant recalls the successful effort of Samuel Whaley Hopkins (town attorney and benefactor), to bring a needed milk factory to Mt. Pleasant and the surrounding community.

In 1906, Hopkins opened joint negotiations with the Ann Arbor railway and the Michigan Condensed Milk Factory of Fairport, New York, to purchase a land parcel from the railroad and to convince the New York-based creamery, owned by the Borden family, to build a factory in Mt. Pleasant. When he returned from New York, having finally succeeded in getting the factory located in Mt. Pleasant, he was met at the train station by the mayor, the Indian School Band and a delegation from the Board of Trade. Hopkins was then escorted to the Bennett Hotel and the opera house, where he told of his victory. Designed by William D. Kyser, Superintendent of the Borden Creamery in Fairport, New York, the creamery was completed in 1908 and operated as a creamery until 1960. The mayor presented him with a new hat, a pocketbook and five twenty dollar gold pieces.

In 1898, chicory manufacturers came to Mt. Pleasant looking for a location for a plant, but put their operation in Port Huron, Michigan. Hopkins kept in touch with them and entered correspondence about the erecting of a plant in Mt. Pleasant. After continued correspondence they came back to Mt. Pleasant and were convinced to locate a plant here.

Poor health continued to plague Hopkins, who died on August 20, 1923, having seen four of his Mt. Pleasant-improving projects go from dream to reality: the Indian Industrial Schools; Central Normal; the sugar beet factory, and the Bordens condensery.

Other than a short winding street in the southwest quadrant of Mt. Pleasant, nothing marks the presence of this dedicated Mt. Pleasant business pioneer, whose legacy dots the town.

CHAPTER 8: SOUTH MISSION

203 South Mission - For many years the Adams Flower Shop near the corner of Mission and Michigan streets was run by Leslie and Helen Adams, then by Helen after Leslie's death. In the early 1980s, the business became Cindy's Flower Boutique and Antiques, owned by Cindy Bigard. In the late 1980s, the building was razed and an Auto parts and repair business in a new building opened on the location, today occupied by a Speedway convenience store and filling station alongside Larry's Automotive Service Center.

307 South Mission - Following ten years of operation in downtown Mt. Pleasant, Dick Shook moved his Western Auto Store to the building formerly occupied by the Greening Service Station and Pickens Repair Shop. In 1985, Shook sold the store to Whitey McCreight, who later moved the business to Weidman. In 1999, a drapery shop was located in the building. The Hobby Shop, Mid-Michigan Upholstery and Awning, and the ICDC (Isabella Child Development Center) Thrift Shop now call the structure home.

404 South Mission - In 1958, Dale Jarrett bought the building that for many years was the White Spot Restaurant, an all night eatery known to local residents by the more familiar title: "the greasy spoon". Apologies to any surviving owners, unflattering as that may be, about a dozen of the author's contemporaries, when questioned while this book was being researched, didn't know where the White Spot was but readily admitted having partaken of late night coffee at the place they knew by the other name. In 2010, the greatly expanded business continues at 406 South Mission, with the old White Spot now the parking lot, under family ownership with Dale's son Mike at the helm.

This is where daddy 181 would walk w/ us from Elizabeth Street on Sunday afternoon

424 South Mission Street was the site of Hubert Brainerd's Dairy, outgrowth of his Orchard Hill Dairy Farm, then Chase's Dairy, inset above. Brainerd's daughter Margaret married Virginian Doug McFarlane in joined her father's growing dairy business. They built a processing plant and opened a dairy bar. Douglas McFarlane bought the business 1942, operating it as Brainerd's until 1948 when the name changed to McFarlane Dairy, above. The dairy bar in the main building, called Chase's for a time, was legendary for it's ice cream concoctions, including a banana split that is still a subject in Mt. Pleasant nostalgic conversations. McFarlane sold the business in 1968 to McDonalds Dairy of Flint, Michigan.

424 South Mission has been the site of the Firehouse Five Car Wash since the mid-1970s.

512 South Mission. – In 1938, Myron Elmore opened his furniture store at this location. At the end of World War II, Myron was joined in the business by his son Stanley, who with wife Lucille, expanded into appliances and ran the growing business until 1984. In 1964, Stan Elmore was one of the first Mt. Pleasant business owners to buy television time on WWTV and do his own live commercials on a Friday night movie program. In 2010, the building is home to Comfort Center.

706-712 South Mission – Following in the meat market footsteps of his father, Loyd, see page 121, Melvin "Dutch" Honeywell, above, and his wife Philomena bought the store at 712 South Mission from Carl and Esther Huber in 1947 renamed it Honeywells. He doubled the size of the building in 1947 and held a grand opening later that year with one side dedicated to groceries and the other side the original meat market. He also added two apartments upstairs, one of which he occupied with his family for three years. Dutch Honeywell bought cattle and hogs from local farmers and various stockyards, did his own slaughtering and butchering, then selling the fresh meat in his store. Honeywell sold the business in 1955. The building was demolished in the late 1960s and was replaced by Domino's Pizza, below.

799 South Mission Street – The building on the northeast corner of Mission and High streets was built by Mr. and Mrs. Kenneth Bandeen in 1939 for business rental. The separate second floor office, accessible from the outside, served as an office for Vic Erler of Vic's Supermarket next door for many years. Northern Auto Supply, was located in the building a forerunner occupant to Post Pharmacy, below, which expanded that business to both floors. It makes no difference to the present time, however, since the address is a parking lot for Ric's Food Center, formerly Vic's, at 705 South Mission. Sid Wheeler was the owner/pharmacist at Post Pharmacy.

816 South Mission began life as Floyd M. Bush's Bush Auto Court, early name by which motels operated to sound a touch classier than tourist cabins, above. Bush sold to Will and Elizabeth Schoder, who sold to Doug and Jane Baird, who eventually sold to Kenneth Wold. Somewhere along

the line the name changed fron Bush's to Reins Motel and was the first Mt. Pleasant Wold's Motel. The property saw it's last motel occupant named the Uptown Motel, right.

In 2010, the motel has been replaced and a commercial building going with an address of 888 South Mission is home to MyGyM, Advance Cash and GameTraders.

901-917 South Mission – The building at 917 South Mission was opened October 25, 1947, as the Hibberd-Tompkins MobilGas Service and Motor Sales, Plymouth and DeSoto dealership. Later, above, it became Central Tire Service, a Goodyear Tire dealer that doubled for many years as the North Star Bus Lines station. Today, the building serves as warehouse space for Assman's Carpets, longtime neighbor next door at 901 South Mission. In 2010, bus service in and out of Mt. Pleasant is handled by Indian Trails at the Blodgett Shell Station, 1911 South Mission

1010-1016 South Mission – In the 1940s, the big white building at the southwest corner of Mission and Gaylord Streets was Stack and Lannen Motor Sales, above. By the 1950s, the building had become Archey Brothers (Carl and "Bud") Motor Sales and Sunoco gasoline filling station. At the far right of the photograph below, across Gaylord Street to the north is the school system's central kitchen, Archey Brothers dealers in American Motors and Oldsmobile cars would eventually move to 706 East Broadway in the 1970s.

1010-1016 South Mission – Before moving further south from 1016 to 1901 South Mission when the former Archey Brothers was razed, Boogie Records and The Other Side, above, were business residents of the building. In the late 1970s, a strip mall was constructed with Spencer Walgreen Drug Store as the anchor store, also occupied for many years by VideoLand, a video rental store. In 2010, the 1010-1016 strip mall is occupied by AutoZone in place of Spencer's, The Mt. Pleasant Sewing Center and Quilt Shop in the VideoLand spot, the newly-opened Mission Street Party Store at 1014 and, the equally new Book Shelf book store at 1012 South Mission.

1017 South Mission – In 1981, the Wagon Wheel fruit and vegetable store, above, occupied this building that was originally built in the 1960s as a Dairy Queen soft ice cream store. Ultimately it became Sempliners Black Tie & Tuxedo Store and is, in 2010, known simply as Black Tie Tuxedo and Costume Shop, below.

1030 South Mission – Longing for the good old days, when you could eat in your car with the radio blasting as your favorite squeeze checked out who was cruising Mission Street? Miss those days …. well, they're still here. *Elaines Cornell brother-in-law*
Jon's Country Burgers drive-in restaurant opened by John P. Spiris June *Bill* 27, 1957, on the northwest corner of Mission and Bellows streets. There were 28 parking spaces alongside two-way speakers where you could order your favorites and there are still 28 spaces where you can do the same.

After an electrical fire in 2000 caused the restaurant to close from April to September, the building was emptied and reconstructed faithful to the original décor inside but with a new sign outside. About the only other thing that has changed since the place opened is the ownership, Jon's is now owned by the founder's son, Jon Spiris, and managed by his son, Mike Spiris, making it three generations of the family serving the same number of generations of Mt. Pleasantites. Would you like fries with that?

1101-1117 South Mission Street – The timeworn print, above, shows Darlene Maxine, Deloris Maricel and Dorothy Mae Davis, in front of their parents, Lawrence and Flossie Davis' D.M.D. Gardens Roller Rink. Darlene Maxine was born in 1939, the year Davis began construction of the building on the land he bought from Paul Lang, a farmer whose land encompassed this area and the location where The Embers restaurant would someday be built. Lawrence Davis dream was to pro- vide a place for good, clean recreation for area citizens, particularly youth, and he named his roller rink D.M.D. Gardens with his daughters' initials in their honor. The rink provided the promised entertainment for more than a generation, drawing skaters from Alma, Beal City, Clare, Farwell, Rosebush and Shepherd. Three of the four daughters met their future husbands at the rink. The rink closed in 1961, and the property was sold to Paul Clabuesch for a Walgreen Drug store, later to become Bill Spencer's first Mt. Pleasant Spencer Walgreen Drug store. In 2010, below, the location is Baumgarth Plaza, providing a business home to Dr. Ashim Aggarwal, dentist Dr. Keith M. Bever, Clay Chiropractic Clinic, Clint Cornell PA-C, Dr. Dan C. Dean D.O, and Mary Stuner C.F.N.P.

1141 South Mission – Here's a case where the then picture and the now one are not all that far apart in age. In 2006, the building, above, was erected as an upscale coffee shop offering onsite-baked goods, light lunches, a variety of coffees, teas, soft drinks and was a Wi-Fi hotspot. When the U.S. economy tanked in 2008, many of the first victims of the bad economy were start-up businesses, including the fledgling Cuppa Joe's. Vacant for nearly two years, property was bought by insurance agent Ryan Schlicht, below, who moved his State Farm Insurance agency here August 1, 2010, from previous offices at 515 North Mission. Schlicht's State Farm agency was started by Earl Richard and continued by Conrad English.

1200 South Mission – Chippewa Lanes shown above in 2000, opened in the late 1950s, with automatic pin setters, a cocktail lounge and state of the art facilities. Bowlers and leagues flocked there then as now. The demise of Pleasant Lanes bowling alley in the late 1960s accelerated the growth of the facility. Below, in 2010, Chippewa Lanes Recreation, owned by Carl Malish, boasts a community room and cocktail lounge. Pleasant Lanes, closed, while out of town on Broomfield Road, Riverview Golf Course got into the bowling alley business and remains so in 2010. In 1959, the University Center at Central Michigan University also had a downstairs bowling alley, which later closed. Then CMU built the Student Activity Center (SAC), including bowling lanes. That about pins-down the Mt. Pleasant bowling scene.

1217 South Mission – The Embers restaurant was the brainchild of Chef Clarence Tuma a Detroit native and Central Michigan College graduate, as well as staffer, was known for its signature "one pound pork chop", which was to draw fine food aficionadas from around the state and the world for great food accompanied by top-notch service and ambiance. The Embers opened its doors to the public March 15, 1958, with hosts Clarence Tuma and Norm LaBelle serving as partners in the operation at the northeast corner of Mission and Bellows streets. In 1967, Tuma bought out the partnership in the restaurant. The kitchen was expanded ion 1961 and a cocktail lounge was added on, later to become a lighter fare restaurant called Tease. The Embers was the undisputed monarch of Mt. Pleasant fine dining for half a century.

Above, just before the Embers opened its doors, Chef Clarence Tuma, center, served more than 600 diners at the Mt. Pleasant Rotary Club First Annual Rotary-sponsored smorgasbord December 1, 1956 and was congratulated for the feat by Rotarians, left to right: William Brown; Don Kilborn; E. Allen Morrow; (Tuma); Emery Johnson; John Rodembeck; and Jack Benford.

1217 South Mission (continued) – The Embers was the site of many banquets, meetings, and individually the place to celebrate any of life's special days.

In 1966, above, the Mt. Pleasant-born supermarket/general merchandise chain, Giant/Giantway celebrated its 25th anniversary at the restaurant, with Chef Tuma showing off a store-shaped cake to Giant President Les Walton and his wife Mildred. The Benford Room was added to the Embers in 1969 and in 1974 another addition was made on the north side of the building.

In 2008, after a half century in business, The Embers closed. In 2010 the building is owned by a young church group.

1400-1418 South Mission was the Stadium Plaza when Mt. Pleasant-based Giant Super Market teamed up with Detroit-based Yankee Stores general merchandise stores to open Mt. Pleasant's first true one-stop shopping venue under one roof June 12, 1963, above. While separate entities, with separate check-outs, the complex nonetheless offered "stay out of the weather" convenience for the food and clothing shopper. Through the years, life changed for both companies. Yankee became K-Mart and opened a store near the corner of Broomfield and Mission while Giant teamed with Giantway to open a shopping center across the street from the Stadium Plaza locale in 1971. Stadium Plaza morphed into the Campus Mall, below, which through a number of owners has seen a variety of businesses come and go like: Spaar Drug and General Store; The Clip Joint; Dino's Pizza; and Montgomery Ward.

1400-1418 South Mission in 2010 is now known as the Campus Plaza occupied by 1400 - Sears Hometown Store, 1414 – MC Sports, just remodeled in August, 2010, 1416 – Menna's Joint, a sandwich shop, and 1418- Sherwin-Williams Paint.

1506 South Mission – "You gotta be nuts to build a hotel way out there. Nobody's gonna stay clear out in the boonies like that." Those were some of the local reactions in 1950 to the proposed hotel for Mission Street, US-27. Having lost the Park and Bennett hotels downtown, Mt. Pleasant was faced with having no upscale commercial lodging. Enter a group of citizens, who formed the Southtown Corporation and sold stock to the public as part of an area-wide fundraiser for construction of a first-class hotel, with the working names of first the "Hi-Way Hotel", then "the Community Hotel", above. Local media breathlessly recounted each step of construction. After an area-wide contest to name the new hostelry, the Chieftain Hotel and Restaurant opened with much pomp and pride in 1951, quickly becoming the center of the city's social life.

1506 South Mission (continued) – Increased competition, chain motels with large meeting venues, fickle public tastes, and time took their tolls on the venerable hotel, below, as the Campus Plaza Inn in 1982.

Several subsequent owners tried to make a go of the aging motel and restaurant complex, but its faded glory remained forever faded. In the last phase of its evolution, the place was known as the Budget Inn, center, until the building was destroyed in 2006. In 2010 the vacant property is flanked by the former Hot 'N Now, now named Oh My!, drive-in restaurant and the Qdoba Mexican Grill, below.

1516 South Mission – The Chieftain Hotel was right across the street when Tommy Falsetta bravely broke ground for Falsetta's Casa Nova

along the residence-dotted US-27 south of town in 1957, gambling that the Falsetta reputation for great Italian food would draw new customers from the hotel and old customers from their downtown location "out in the country".

Tom and Tony Falsetta opened their first bar and restaurant at 111 West Broadway, later the Moose Club, then moved to 221 North Main Street before moving to this Mission Street location.

1516 South Mission (continued) – The Falsetta's decision to open the Casa Nova on South Mission proved to be a good one, as the business continually expanded. The addition of the University Room made Falsetta's a destination for a number of civic club meetings. In February 1986, Falsetta's Casa Nova closed. Tony Falsetta died in 1987 and Tom died in 1993. Since the late 1980s, the location has been home to another ethnic food establishment, the La Senorita Mexican Restaurant.

1530 South Mission Street - After humble beginnings in a small building at 711 East Bellows, left, just west behind Jon's Drive-in, C & O T-Shirts moved to their present location in 1981, above, the former Appliance Center location. In 2010, as C & O Sportswear, the business boasts expanded merchandise selection, and modernized apartment neighbors.

1623 South Mission – In 1964, Hall Brothers built a new Sunoco gasoline filling station at this location, above, which was then 3748 South Mission Road since it was not yet in the city limits, and moved from their station at the corner of Broomfield and Mission. In 1974, they sold the property to a developer and moved offices to the Taylor Building downtown. In 2010, the station is the anchor for the Campus Court Shopping Center containing: B-Tan, Cellular One, Fit 4 U, Morningstar Bakery, Pita Pit, Shin's Korean Restaurant, the Side Door, a Subway shop, and the U.S. Armed Services Recruiting Station.

1623 South Mission – Originally the site of the Pixie South, with the same menu as the flagship Pixie Drive In on North Mission, this larger, more modern version of the Pixie brought the signature Coney Island hotdog to residents of the south side of town in the mid-1960s. A decade later, LaBelle Enterprises President Bart LaBelle made the long circulated rumor "We're going to get a Big Boy here" come true by re-tooling the Pixie South building into a Big Boy restaurant, which continues operation in 2010.

1707-1721 South Mission – Above is a poorly reproduced photo from a newspaper ad touting the November 10, 1971, opening of the Giant-Giantway Plaza in the 1700 block of South Mission. It was the best we could do after searching files. Anyway, it was a pretty big deal. Long before the Wal-Marts, K-Marts, Meijers, Targets and other super stores hit town, we had our own homegrown Giant Super Market chain, operations deftly managed by Shirley Martin Decker, who remains in 2010 as an enthusiastic booster of all things Mt. Pleasant. The mega superstore had satellite businesses within the building and was, in fact, the first Mt. Pleasant home of Robaire's Bakery. Eventually the Giant-Giantway chain folded in the face of competition from super super stores.

In 2010 the complex, now known as the Central Square Shopping Center, is home to: 1705 - R & R Laundry; 1707 – Liquor 1; 1711 - China 1 Buffet; 1713 - Save-A-Lot food store; 1717 Salvation Army Thrift Shop; 1719 - Check America Cash Advance; 1721 – Family Dollar; and 1723 – Soldan's feeds and pet supplies. In July, 2010, owners plan an additional 5,000 square foot shopping center for the parking lot.

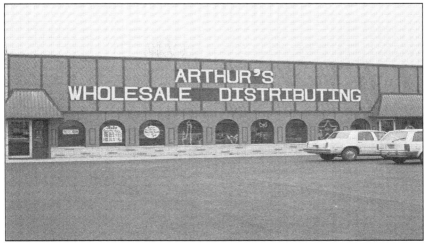

1805 South Mission Street - Since beginning life in the late 1950s as a short-lived roller skating rink, this building has been occupied by business enterprises of the Silverberg family since the early 1960s, when Arthur Silverberg opened Dart Discount, the first general merchandise, with emphasis on clothing, discount retail operation in Mt. Pleasant. The operation evolved to meet changing marketing conditions to become Arthur's Catalogue Showroom and Arthur's Jeweler's Exchange, then Arthur's Wholesale Distributing later, above in 1982.

In 2010, above, Steve Silverberg continues the two generation family tradition at the 1805 South Mission location with S. Silverberg Finer Jewelers, above, in a complex that has expanded to include: Michigan Works; Sinister Productions Tattoos; Designer Consignor; and, Sue Nault's Paperback Book Exchange.

1911 South Mission Street – The northeast corner of Mission and Broomfield roads, above, was for many years a gasoline service station with tourist cabins out behind. When motorists came to Mt. Pleasant from the south on two-lane U.S. 27, these were the first accomodations they encountered. In 1964, Lyle and Harlan "Bones" Hall bought the property from Albert Schertel. The Halls operated from this location until building a new service station at 1620 S. Mission in 1964.

Below, the Hall Brothers wrecker is shown, not necessarily because it was a unique piece of equipment but in the background, left, is the home of Ken Helber, at 1912 South Mission Road, owner of Log Cabin Record Shop, right, at 1908 South Mission, a Mt. Pleasant institution for decades, until the early 1970s.

1908 South Mission Street – By the late 1970s Ken Helber's home at 1912 South Mission was the first to go, replaced by a Burger King, parking lot left, when his Log Cabin Record Shop, by that time owned by Tom Barr, was replaced by the Mt. Pleasant branch of Chemical Bank. Chemical State Bank, cornerstone office of the bank holding company, opened in Midland, Michigan, in 1871. The headquarters of Chemical Bank was the scene of a September 29, 1937, bank robbery at the hands of career criminal Tony Chebatoris and fellow prison inmate Jack Gracey. During the robbery, truck driver Henry Porter of Bay City was shot and killed when Chebatoris mistook him for a police officer. Chebatoris was sentenced to death for the crime and executed in 1938 by federal authorities. Below, the Mt. Pleasant office looks much the same in 2010, with the exception of a healthy growth of trees. Chemical Financial Corporation, name of the ten affiliate bank, 87 branch office holding company was named in 2005. Burger King is still next door in 2010.

2000 South Mission Street – Other early then South Mission Road, business pioneers were Dick and Wilma Anderson, who in 1950 built their Pleasant Lane bowling alley "clear out in the wilds" of Broomfield and Mission, above. Suddenly Mt. Pleasant has two bowling alleys. one over a storefront on South Main and this state of the art facility. Automatic pinsetters were years away when the author hand set pins for the late leagues in the early 50s. The walk home to the West Side through the dark of the field from Broomfield and Mission to Preston and Washington, where the first street light north was located ... Washington south of Preston holding only a few residents, railroad tracks and three migrant worker summer season only occupied houses ... was punctuated only by the occasional stumble over holes in the then open field.

That field is now paved and lighted and clustered with Central Michigan University buildings.

Pleasant Lanes closed in the mid-1960s, trumped by the more modern facilities of Chippewa Lanes at 1200 South Mission.

In 2010, above, Wayside Central and O'Kelly's Pub occupy the address.

2003 - 2015 South Mission Street – Sweeney Seed Company pioneered the southeast corner of Broomfield and Mission roads, above, as a business location in the 1960s, eventually closing the site in favor of their downtown location on South Washington Street. Payless Shoes has been the anchor ever since, with Elliott's Greenhouse's second location for awhile and BoRics hair care in the south half of the two-store mini-complex in 2010. Below, built in the 1980s just south of the Broomfield Road and Mission Street intersection, the House of Flavors menu offered a full selection of meals. It's "way out in the country" location was compensated by the K-Mart located next door, representing the first reach of the commerce corridor south of the Broomfield/Mission crossroads. The restaurant closed in the 1980s, but was promptly converted to C & S Engraving for many years and more recently a "mini-mall", below, including Liberty Tax Services, the Campus Salon and Game Trader. The building was demolished in early 2010 as part of a Firstbank expansion from next door to the north.

4097 East Blue Grass Road – For 51 years, WCEN 1150 AM was the radio voice of Mt. Pleasant. Beginning August 8, 1949, WCEN, under the ownership of Mt. Pleasant's Paul Brandt, started broadcasting from 112½ East Broadway, over Voisin's Jewelry Store. In 1953, the broadcast studio moved "way out in the country" to Blue Grass Road, where a three-tower directional array had been constructed the year before. The station, now with 94.5 AM, sold to Central Michigan Broadcasting, with Charles Anthony principal owner General Manager, in February, 1968. Richard Sommerville purchased WCEN AM & FM in May, 1986, and sold the stations in November 2000. WCEN FM was then moved to Saginaw while WCEN-AM made its last broadcast that same month.

The WCEN site, above, has become the location of Mt. Pleasant's Target store below, while WCEN-FM 94.5 is still broadcasting from Saginaw.

Mt. Pleasant-based radio stations in 2010 are: WCFX - 95.3 FM; WCMU Public Broadcasting - 89.5 FM; WCZY - 104.3 FM; WMMI-830 AM; and WUPS-98.5 FM.

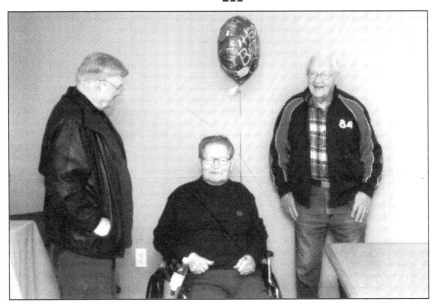

4097 East Blue Grass Road (continued). -Voices from Mt. Pleasant's radio past. – At the December 29, 2009, birthday gathering for 40 year Mid-Michigan broadcaster Jim Hughes, seated center above, fellow past broadcasters Jim Jennings, left, and Duane Allen wished the legendary WCEN personality many more. Below, Hughes and longtime WCEN broadcaster Gary Bugh recall fellow WCENers, including Chuck Anthony, Jim Bailey, Donner Bailey, Bob Banta, Dan Bethel, Dick Bing, Dan Bragg, Ken Burlington, Paul Carey, Mike Carey, Rheba Dedie, Dick Enberg, Pete Fronczak, Dan Hole, Neal Johnson, Joe Kinosky, Georgia Martin, Coleman Peters, Frank Robinson, Chet Rogoza, Tina Sawyer, Dan Smith, Gary Sole, Chuck Stevens, Gene Umlor, Larry Wentworth, Wendy Wood, Lou Williams, Harold Zeoli and Winona Zoleski.

CHAPTER 9: MT. PLEASANT IN THE 1920s:

(NOTE: The following narrative was written by Mt. Pleasant High School student Phil G. Collin and was found, along with accompanying photographs, in a metal box in the cornerstone of the old high school (then the Junior High School) at 300 South Fancher Street when that building was razed to allow construction of today's Sacred Heart Catholic Church. The essay was reprinted in the Mt. Pleasant Daily Times News April 14, 1967 –ed.)

THE CITY OF MT. PLEASANT
AS IT APPEARED IN 1920
By Phil G. Collin

Before beginning this description let me explain the purpose at which it aims. Its chief purpose is to correctly inform and satisfy the curiosity of the future residents of this city. At the time in which this will be read, Mt. Pleasant will probably be far different from the present city.

Its streets will be longer and steps will have been taken to beautify them. New stores and other buildings will have sprung up here and there where now only vacant lots appear, and the city will undoubtedly be greatly changed. Many things written herein may seem interesting and many others humorous but nevertheless its humor is unintended at the present time and its sole purpose is to interest you for awhile and perhaps bring back the picture of Mt. Pleasant way back in 1920.

The city extends northward to the present Chicory Plant and its southern extremity is marked by the Central Michigan Normal School Campus. Mission and Harris Streets determine its east and west boundaries respectively.

Mt. Pleasant, like all Gaul, is divided into three distinct segments: business district, industrial, and residential. The business district occupies chiefly Main Street and Broadway extending on the former from the elevator and offices of H.E. Chatterton and son to Illinois Street and on the latter from the Ann Arbor Depot to Lansing Street. A brief description of the business district will suffice. The most important of the establishments are R. O. Doughty's and C. E. Hagen's dry goods stores, two men's clothing stores owned by W. E. Lewis, Kane and Kane and Chas. Woodruff, the Olympia Candy Works, grocery stores of Martin Welch, J. A. Kinney, Frank Sweeney, Morton and Simonds, and Henry Breidenstein.

The leading of the many drug stores with which Mt. Pleasant is supplied are those of E. E. Palmer, Gray and Lathrop, P.C. Taylor, S. MacCarthy and G. H. MacGillivray. Jewelry stores are owned by George Foland and F.L. Klunzinger. The leading photo studios are those of E. F. Collins, H. Francisco and H. Bellinger's.

Mt. Pleasant possesses three newspapers: the Times, the Enterprise and the Courier. Each of these publishes a weekly edition and each also has a fat subscription list. The situation of these offices and shop are as follows: the Times is located on West Broadway between Main Street and Harris' Mill. The Enterprise occupies a position directly back of the Isabella County State Bank on South Normal Avenue, while the Courier is situated in the center of the 200-300 Block of South Main Street.

This city boasts of two reliable banks. One is the Isabella County State Bank located on the corner of Broadway and Normal Avenue at the Northern termination of the latter, directly opposite Marsh and Graham's dry goods store which is also one of the leading stores in its Line.

The other bank referred to is the Exchange Savings Bank on the southeast corner of the intersection of Broadway and Main Street. It occupies a large white stone building and its slogan is "The Bank on the Busy Corner" that of the Isabella being "The Bank of Personal Service". Either slogan could well apply to both.

We have at present ten doctors, and four dentists, whose offices are either over the business blocks mentioned or scattered throughout the residential district. Six lawyers ply their trades in this city and their offices also are over the business blocks. The Park and Bennett Hotels, located on the corners of Main and Broadway, and Broadway and Court Street respectively are the two leading ones.

A new theater, the Broadway, located as its name implies on one of the main streets together with the Lyric afford Mt. Pleasant motion picture entertainment. I guess I have mentioned every butcher, baker and electric light maker here and a short exposition on the industries of this will not be amiss.

Mt. Pleasant has just sailed out on its manufacturing or industrial career in the form of the Transport Truck Co. Although the Borden Condensed Milk Factory, the Chicory Plant, Harris Milling Co., Mt. Pleasant Lumber Company or A. E. Gorham have existed here for several years they have never marked the city as a manufacturing one.

The Transport Truck Co., however, although in its infancy, has placed Mt. Pleasant on the industrial map and its product is distributed by dealers throughout the country. Its one factory is located in the north western extremity of the city adjacent to the Riverside Cemetery and the Indian School. With its present capacity, it is completing ten trucks a day and steps are soon to be taken to increase this amount to between 15 and 30. It is considered to be Mt. Pleasant's most important industry and the citizens stand back of it in every way.

The Columbia Sugar Beet Company is rapidly completing the erection of a plant started many years ago. The latter having failed, the building was left in a state of half completion and has for years been an eyesore to the citizens until the present company took the reins in 1919 and is now nearly ready to install machinery. It is hoped by all that this industry together with the Transport Truck and the Dow Chemical works north of the city will be great assets to the community.

The Public buildings are the County Court House, Jail and Sheriff's residence, occupying the square just north of Broadway between Main and Court Street, "two of which buildings are in use", the Rest Room, a small building adjacent on the north, to the Park Hotel, the Fire Station and City Clerk's office on the corner of South Normal and Michigan, and the Library on East Broadway.

The public school system contains the Kinney School on North Kinney, the Fancher School on West Maple Street, the Junior High School on South Fancher and the High School proper which is at present occupying various rooms at the Central Michigan Normal School during the process of erection of the new High School adjacent to the Junior High on South Fancher. The West Side School across the river is also a part of the system.

The State owns the Central Michigan Normal School buildings at the southern extremity of Normal Avenue. This institution possessed five buildings, namely the Normal building in

1895 or thereabouts, the gymnasium, the Science Building, the Training School, and the heating plant.

The Training School contains the grades from the first through the eighth, where Normal Students receive practical teaching experience.

But if Mt. Pleasant is blessed with schools it is doubly blessed with churches. The Presbyterian and the Methodist located on South Main Street, the Church of Christ and the Baptist on East Broadway, the Catholic on East Illinois Street and the Christian Science on South Normal Avenue constitute the most important of these.

Four new buildings have been recently built among which are Bamber's Garage on East Broadway and the Broadway Theater, while the Government Post Office and the new Public High School are still under construction.

Two railroads, the Ann Arbor and the Pere Marquette afford transportation facilities, the former passing through Mt. Pleasant while a branch of the latter terminates here.

The streets are long and wide and beautiful shade trees (set out by the early residents) and many beautiful residences, line them. Plans are already in formulation for a systematic arrangement of shrubbery and plans for a city of beauty, as well as one of commercial value are being formed.

Rich farm lands surround the city and although its size is at present small, the population being 7,000, a steady moderate growth is foreseen free from any temporary "booms".

Accompanying this description are several photographs which although of slight value now will be curiosity indeed in the years to come if well preserved. Hence this little attempt at a description of the best town in Michigan – Mr. Pleasant.

Phil G. Collins, sophomore
Mt. Pleasant High School
1920

CHAPTER 10: WEST SIDE

200 West Broadway – Built early in the 20th Century as the Isabella County Farmers Grain and Bean Company, the business was bought in 1928 by Howard Renwick Barryton from Will Francis. In 1963, above, the building suffered a fire and Renwick decided not to rebuild. The building was destroyed in 1967 by a "controlled burn" by the Mt. Pleasant Fire Department. In 2010, the site is part of the parking lot for the City-owned Riverside Apartments, below.

201-203 West Broadway - The Smithers Building, built in 1911, has been home to many businesses but was apparently empty in this 1950s photograph. See previous page for 1930s occupants. In the 1940s, Marianne Style Center and Prior's Montgomery Ward called the building home; followed in the 1950s by LaPonte's Bar, forerunner of Freddies; then by Mt. Pleasant Beauty School, now M. J. Murphy Beauty School in 2010, below. In the 1950s, as in 2010, Sweeney Seed Company peeks out from behind the Smithers Building on Washington Street.

The 200 block of West Broadway (continued) - This is the same block as on the previous page viewed from the opposite direction, looking from the west. In 2010, above, left to right, occupancy of the block includes; 205 – Computers; 207-209 the Halloween Store; and 211- Heart Strings and Fun Things. Through the years, the block has been occupied by Ray Cline Marketing, Francisco Photograpic Studio, Grinzinger Insurance, Jagger's Shoe Service, John's Inn restaurant, Plant Parenthood, Prior's Montgomery Ward Store, Roethlisberger Real Estate, and Shorty's Shoe Repair. Below, the former *Isabella County Times,* the *Times-News* newspaper offices at 215-217 West Broadway has variously been occupied by attorney's offices, Toberson's Plumbing and Heating, Superior Toberson Heating and Cooling, and the U.S. Health, Education and Welfare Department and Social Security Administration offices. Dr. Larry Bennett's and Dr. McClure's offices occupy the building in 2010.

304 -312 West Michigan Street – Built by N. D. Gover in 1936 and remodeled dramatically 20 years later by son Bob Gover, this mammoth building was once all one dry goods, clothing and merchantile store. N. D. Gover passed away in 1974. Son Bob opened Gover City Fabrics at 221 West Michigan, below, where Wilderness Outfitter is now located, in 1980. In 2010, the building is home to MAC 3 TV, Centennial Hall – where the Mt. Pleasant Elks Club once met, along with A & D Home Health Care, American Red Cross, Bassett Transportation, Big Brothers/Big Sisters, Christian Counseling Service, Massage at its Best, Reasonable Hearing, Wyeth Pharmaceutical, and Neat 'N Clean,

200 Walnut Street - Above, Fred West, Frances Sowle, Harold Sowle with Sidney Sowle holding Theo Sowle in front of the Sowle family home at 213 Walnut Street, Sidney Sowle & Son, Inc. movers has its roots in the early 1900s when Sidney Sowle and Andy Cuthbert started a two-man moving business. When Cuthbert died in 1911, Sowle became the only owner of the business, which grew rapidly. In 1919, Sowle bought the first Transport moving truck, inset below. In 1932, the company became affiliated with Mayflower Moving, and in 1945, after World War II, Theo "Sid" Sowle joined his father in the business. The original Sid Sowle died in 1953 and William Sowle, his grandson, joined the firm in 1957, rising to company president. Below, the company's home until the 1990s on Mill Street. The company is now Mayflower Transit Agency at 515 Industrial Avenue. In 2009, Mayflower honored the company as a 45-year agent.

411 West Broadway - William E. and John A. Harris, sons of William S. and Sarah Harris of London, England, by way of Montcalm County, Michigan, bought the mill site, cleared timber and built their first mill on West Broadway in 1872. The Chippewa River had already been dammed by Harper Brothers in 1866 to provide power for a saw mill. The original log and dirt dam was replaced by a cement dam and a mill race was dug to the mill. Mill stones were used until about 1915 to grind feed and graham flour. In 1930, the Harris's installed a water-driven electric plant and bought electric power when the river was low, selling electricity to the same company when the river was high. An electric substation still exists just west of the mill site. Above, Harris Mill from the back in 1906. Below, a few years later a sleek new tower had been built when the electric plant was installed.

411 West Broadway (continued) - The back of Harris Milling Company in 1938. About 1915, the Harris brothers started producing a prepared pancake mix and in the 1930s, a prepared biscuit mix. Other specialty products added later were dog food, dairy, trout and turkey feed. Those

specialty foods were marketed under the name Famo. In 1966, the Harris Mill was sold to Conagara, who sold to Honeggar Feed Company. Left is a picture of the back of the mill after the mill run was closed in the 1970s, The mill closed in the mid-1980s.

411 West Broadway (continued) – The Sunday evening, October 28, 1990, night sky was aglow with the blaze in the vacant former Harris Milling Company building, above, as a fire of unknown origin gutted the 118-year-old structure, boarded up just the week before.The fire was so intense that a utility pole across the street burst into flames while baseball-sized ashes fell on homes and businesses as far away as High Street, half a mile distant and lights melted from fire trucks 100 feet from the blaze.

The gutted building sat empty nearly a decade. After a long period of abandonment, the fire-ravaged former Harris Milling Company building met the wrecking ball in 1999, 127 years after the company's start in 1872. Two-foot thick walls and an estimated $200,000 to $300,000 cost to tear the building down delayed it's leveling.

411 West Broadway (continued) – On the site of the old Harris Milling Company building in 2010 is David Mc Guire's complex of offices and apartments occupying the entire 400 block of West Broadway and south along Mill Street to Walnut Street. Note the Consumers Power electric substation at the far end of the parking lot, a remnant of the days when that company and Harris Milling swapped electric power. The office complex facing West Broadway includes: Gratiot Health Services and Broadway Health Services on the ground floor with apartments and a meeting room on the second level. Below, the McGuire complex is viewed from the back. Compare this view with the 1938 and 1971 images on a previous page.

412 West Broadway – The customers of the new Mt. Pleasant Lumber Company, opened in 1914, above, take advantage of January 12, 1915, good sleighing weather to buy and haul away spring building materials. Independent Milling Company can be seen to the right, while the lower left shows part of the bridge over the mill-run to the Chippewa River, with its new canal on the west side of the former Fancher's Meadows forming Island Park. Below, same scene ninety-five and one-half years later in 2010, with the old millrun now a parking lot and the Independent Mill site an open field awaiting completion of the recession-delayed West Broadway Revitalization Project Phase II erection of planned condominiums.

506 West Broadway – The Ann Arbor Railroad came to Mt. Pleasant in 1885 from the south, six years after the Pere Marquette line from Coleman connected the town to the outside world by rail from the northeast. The Ann Arbor line gave a more direct route to the village from larger poulation centers to the south and a regular schedule made rail travel common, as in this 1915 photo, above. In 2010, the Mountain Town Station Brewery and Steakhouse, below, has become as much an important staple to Mt. Pleasant as the railroad was in the past. 2010 Mt. Pleasant Mayor Jim Holton owns the Mountain Town Station.

West Broadway Bridge over the Chippewa River – Following the 1910 collapse of a wooden bridge spanning the Chippewa River just west of the Ann Arbor depot on West Broadway, a new cement bridge was constructed, above. When it was built, Mt. Pleasant was able to boast having the longest cement span bridge in Michigan. The title didn't last long, but enthusiatic Mt. Pleasant boosters snapped up "Longest Span" post cards, origin of the above scene, as soon as they were printed to send to potenial newcomers. In 2010, refurbished, reinforced and repainted many times, the bridge continues to serve, but with the clop-clop of horse traffic replaced by the whisper of automobile tires.

600-700 West Broadway – Two of Mt. Pleasant's oldest outdoor City-maintained venues are represented in this 1910 photograph of the vault at the east perimeter of the Riverside cemetery, which could be accessed by the road approach through Nelson Park. We'll talk more about Nelson Park in the "Parks and Memorials" chapter of this book. Riverside Cemetery is a municipal facility operated and maintained by the City of Mt. Pleasant. Two city departments combine efforts to assure smooth operation of the cemetery. The City Clerk's office handles: cemetery records, space and lot sales, burial arrangements, and foundations. The Parks and Recreation Department handles: cemetery maintenance, burials, landscaping, rules, and fall/spring clean-up. Below, same scene in 2010.

714 West Broadway - The north perimeter of Riverside Cemetery was the 1915 site of construction of a mausoleum by Rome Flannery, far right, and a work crew for the Flowers Mausoleum Company. The mausoleum was built to hold 168 crypts. In 2010, there are 142 burials in the mausoleum, with 24 additional crypts sold, and 2 crypts unsold. The earliest burial recorded in the mausoleum was 1916, with the most recent being in August of 2000. When Flowers Mausoleum Company dissolved, the City of Mt. Pleasant received a Quit Claim Deed in 1964 for the mausoleum and has owned, operated, and maintained the building since. In 2010, below, mausoleum is regularly closed year round, except certain hours during the Memorial Day holiday weekend.

800 West Broadway – In the 1890s, this address belonged to Henry Caple's chicken farm. Around the turn of the 19th Century, Henry changed from chickens to flowers, opening the Mt. Pleasant Greenhouse. In 1945, young Kenneth Elliott came home from World War II and married Caple's daughter, Maxine. Within a year, Ken and Maxine bought the greenhouse, which saw the name changed to Elliott's Greenhouse, a name that's lasted more than five and a half decades at this writing. The Elliott's were prime movers on Mt. Pleasant social and civic scene for many years. Son Paul Elliott, who lent us the above 1952 picture off his office wall, is owner/operator of Elliott's Greenhouse, below, in 2010.

801-805 West Broadway – A night shot is the only photo of the West Side Hobby Shop available, owing to a fire that destroyed the records of the last owners, Ernest Lynn and Valerie Wolters. The Wolters bought the business from Elmer and Elizabeth Flaugher in 1972. The log-sided building was alongside the Chippewa River at the east side of Flaugher's home at 805 West Broadway. Initially the structure was home to Flaughers plumbing and heating business, but he moved that to his expanded garage and the original hobby shop opened there. The inset to the above photo is a view of the shop, with a really neat fireplace, and some of the remote control airplane kits they sold. In 1976, the Wolters moved the business to the former Waters Shoe Store location at 126 South Main Street, where it operated into the 1990s. Below, since 2007, the 801-805 West Broadway location has been home to River's Bluff, a townhouse complex for seniors, with two level townhouses all facing the river.

1101 West Broadway - Nagy's Refinery Service on the southwest corner of Broadway and Harris streets on Mt. Pleasant's west side. Mike "Milo" Nagy owned and operated the business from the mid-1950s until his retirement in 1968. The building has served a variety of businesses and was for a time a private residence. Since the Nagy era, the site has been Lynn Jones gasoline and service station, Jack West's Used Car Sales and is most recently the home of J & B Used Cars. Nagy perished in a boating accident at Brimley in Michigan's Upper Peninsula May 1, 1986.

1021 West Broadway – Christopher and Margurite Graham Torpey built a family grocery/gas station/meat market here in 1930, then added living quarters with a kitchen to the back of the building. Below on the porch of the large back yard is Christopher, with daughters Virginia and Susanne.

1021 West Broadway (continued) – A 1940s addition to the east side of the building at first was used for storage. Later the addition was home to Otterbine's Barber Shop, Tillie's Restaurant, and others. In 1963, Christopher Torpey sold the property to Mike Nagy, who converted it to a coin laundry. More recently the building has housed the now defunct Crystal Pure Lindsey Soft Water dealer.

1018 West Broadway – In the 1940s, it was Milo Jones Grocery on the west side of the building, with Lawrence Tanner's Shell gasoline filling station on the east side and Mr. Tanner's candy shop and post office in the middle. Following Jones death in 1966, the store was bought by Luigi "Louie" Deni. Deni sold the building and business in 1980, above with The Toleing Belle on the east side, and the grocery closed in 1987. In 2010 the building is vacant except for Robin Hood's Barbeque take-out, below.

1101 West Broadway – Originally the First Church of the Nazarene, established in the mid-1930s at the southwest corner of Broadway and Livingston streets, the church added the western wing in 1949. In the mid-1970s the congregation built a new church on south Lincoln Road. The Central Baptist Church moved into the building in 1982. Above, the church in 2010, with Pastor Gordon Rydman presiding.

1101 West Broadway – The West Side Barber Shop, Dave Brown- since 1972, and West Side Beauty Shop, Jane Cotter – since 1971, share this building, constructed by Corbett & Greenwald in the 1950s with Don Wade as the first barber here, followed by Bill Kennedy and Keith Cook. Verdine Wade the first beautician.

1202 West Broadway – In 1937, Ray Doerr started his sheet metal business in his garage, expanding into Doerr Heating and Cooling and expanding into an addition built on the north side of the property. Founder Ray Doerr died in 1964. In 1993, son Ron Doerr, who operated the business after his father's death, sold the business, which was moved to 1215 South Mission Road, at Mt. Pleasant's north city limits, where the operation continues in 2010.

1208 West Broadway – In the early 1940s, this small house was the home of C. W. "Cliff" Collin, yeah the guy with eleven kids, but only five then. When his family outgrew the house, Cliff moved to 326 North Fancher. Later occupants included former one-room school teacher Elsie Emery when she taught at Ganiard School.

302 South Adams - The original four-room West Side School was built in the 1890s to accommodate first through seventh grade elementary school students living across the Chippewa River. This school became known as the Ganiard School Annex when the roomier Ganiard School opened across the street and two blocks north on Adams in 1934. "The Annex" became an apartment house in the 1940s and remains so in 2010.

101 South Adams - Ganiard School, above, was built in 1934 as an early project of President Franklin Delano Roosevelt's Works Progress Administration (WPA) program. It was dedicated on Valentine's Day, 1935. The school and playground occupied the entire 100 block of South Adams Street and most of the 100 South Livingston Street behind the school. Named for 1914-1939 Mt. Pleasant Superintendent of Schools George E. Ganiard, the school initially taught Kindergarten through 6th Grade. Additions in 1950, and the 1970s extended the building further southward. With the original Ganiard School in 2010 still anchoring the

complex near the Broadway at Adams corner, is home to over 375 students and occupies most of the 100 block of Adams Street facing.

302 South Adams (continued) -The Ganiard School Carnival in the autumn of each year draws students, parents, alumni and friends back to Ganiard for games, prizes, drawings, and refreshments, as in 1958 above. On May 27, 2010, a 75th Ganiard School Birthday Celebration was held in the school gym, drawing more than 300 people. Retired Ganiard First Grade teacher and Ganiard History Project (*Ganiardhistory08 @gmail.com*) Co-coordinator Val Wolters, holding the microphone, showed and sold a DVD of the school's history, with proceeds going to the Ganiard History Project Scholarship Fund.

700-702 South Adams – The West Side most active senior Ambassador is Bill Burden, who turned 103-years old in August, 2010. He celebrated the week by "sidewalk superintending" the re-paving and curbing of High Street.

Bill Burden stands between the two South Adams Street houses he has alternately called home since 1930.

When Bill Burden moved to 702 South Adams Street in 1930 there was no water, sewer, or electric service in 1930, the High Street Bridge crossing the Chippewa River was still eight years away and getting to downtown Mt. Pleasant involved a circuitous route seven blocks south to Broadway Street, the nearest bridge to go east.

Born in Ohio in 1907, young Burden was a rig builder there before coming to Michigan at 23 years old when the lure of the prolific Mt. Pleasant Oilfield was providing work in the job-starved Great Depression. He moved away, got married and came back to buy the house at 700 South Adams for $700.00 in 1933. He has lived there ever since. "When we first moved here we had a clear view across the millpond and the trains coming through on the other side." Bill says. A clever tinkerer and innovator, he built a model drilling rig in 1934 for the 1935 Michigan Oil and Gas Exposition in 1935 and traveled the state with the model in a special-built trailer to fairs and exposition throughout Michigan

Jack-of-all trades, Bill left the oilfields when World War II slowed the oil business to a temporary crawl as men and materials went to the war

Marie and Bill Burden look over the newly refurbished oil rig model Bill built in the 1930s October 9, 2009, with daughter Betty (Coomer) and son Don. Don did the model reconstruction work.

effort. He was in the construction business for many years, working on such projects as Ganiard School, Barnes and Barnard Halls at Central

Michigan College and the Frank Lloyd Wright-designed house and church in nearby Alma, Michigan. It is part of local oral legend that Bill figured out how to curve the wood for the pews in the church to conform to Wright's design.

For many years after retirement nearly four decades ago, Bill pursued his hobbies, amongst which were building motorcycles, tractors and scooters. Any nearby construction, including the building of the pavilion for Millpond Park, the Isabella Community Soup Kitchen and Freddie's Tavern across the street, as well as all the millpond landfill businesses facing High Street, found Bill front row center to watch. He's still the "go to guy" if the Soup Kitchen encounters a construction problem to be troubleshot.

With his wife, of nearly 80 years, Marie, Burden lives in Michigan summers and in Florida winters, while keeping in touch with the world via the internet. Yeah, he's made himself computer literate.

Still ready to discuss events of yesterday or three quarters of a century ago with equal sharpness and lucidity of detail with any and all, Bill's mobility has been slowed only slightly by age and a recent need for a stint in the heart, doctors thought he was about eighty when they operated early in 2010 in Florida. But he uses the motorized wheelchair sparingly, walking most of the time. In early 2009, when the author visited him in Florida, he had just come off the roof from trimming an overhanging tree branch that annoyed him.

"Across the dirt road it was just empty field and the millpond when we moved here" Bill told us early in the summer of 2010.

Bill Burden, Mt. Pleasant's own Energizer Bunny ... he just keeps goin', and goin', and goin'.

621 South Adams. - The Isabella Community Soup Kitchen became a class project of Gary Taylor while he was a student at Central Michigan University in 1990. Gary witnessed a fellow student from China eating a ketchup sandwich, the only food available to him at that time, since the country sponsoring his stay in the United States only furnished funds for books, material, room and board but not much else for food.

Gary found no Soup Kitchen in the area and began creating one. The Wesley Foundation at CMU agreed to provide a kitchen and cafeteria. As word of the kitchen spread, more and more people came to the Soup Kitchen. In 1993, Gary found a larger facility when Trinity United Methodist Church at 202 Elizabeth Street offered its basement, where the Soup Kitchen operated for nearly ten years. Again the Soup Kitchen needed more space and the church also needed room for its programs.

A site was found to construct a new building. The new Soup Kitchen, above, with Director Genny Sobaski in front, opened its doors in December 2002. In 2003, former Soup Kitchen Lead Cook, Janet Stenman, an original volunteer, bequeathed a donation that helped pay off the Kitchen's mortgage.

Soup Kitchen patrons come from all walks of life: the homeless; retired people; lonely widowers unable to cook; CMU students living on a low budget; people with low paying jobs; and single parents with children; those unable to hold a job due to physical or mental illness; and young couples with small children newly relocated to the area and need a hand to get started.

The Soup Kitchen receives no government money, operation and maintenance of the facility is completely from donations by individual and corporate members of the community.

In 2010, on the average, 2,150 hot lunches are served monthly, numbers increasing during the summer. The Soup Kitchen doors are open seven days a week, year around.

705 South Adams. – The first half of this building was built by Cyrl LaPointe when he moved his bar from the Smithers Building at the corner of Broadway and Washington in 1968. E. J. Tessine added onto the building in 1972 and operated the bar as E. J.s. In 1981, Fred Phillips II bought the business and the name has been Freddie's Neighborhood Tavern to 2010, above, with full food service including broasted chicken.

808 South Adams – The exterior of Coca Cola Bottling Company of Mt. Pleasant has added to many times since in 1930s construction. No longer a bottling plant, the company distributes Coca Cola products it receives from Grand Rapids. Brick from the old Methodist Church on South Main Street is reportedly buried under the north parking lot.

200-900 West High Street – In 1920, Michigan highway M-20 was routed from Bay City to Ludington by way of Clare and Reed City. In 1926 the route was redesignated as US 10 and the M-20 designation was assigned a route roughly the same as today's, from Midland through Mt. Pleasant, Big Rapids, White Cloud to Muskegon. The route brought the highway from Remus to Bradley Street in Mt. Pleasant, where it was routed north to Broadway Street, then east through town to Shepherd Road and north to the present M-20 to Midland In 1938, the State Highway Department approved a new routing of West M-20 along West High Street through Mt. Pleasant, including and extension of West High Street,with a huge trenching job done to a bridge and fill across the Chippewa River millpond, above in 2010. A trestle across High was built for the Ann Arbor railroad crossing, below. The work was started in late 1938 but suspended during the winter to be resumed in April of 1939 and completed later that year. Since then to 2010 the road has expanded from two lanes to four, the bridge over the river expanded and remodeled several times, now including sidewalk on the north side and a motorless trail extension on the south side.

1114 West High Street. – One of the first buildings erected on the reclaimed land from the millpond fill project on West High Street was Wentworth IGA, built by Charles Wentworth, who ultimately went on to build a Holiday Inn hotel at Houghton Lake. Through a number of name convolutions, always as a food store, the location was joined on the land strip by PaPa Don's restaurant, a bank, a sports store named Big Boy's Toys, a hardware store first called Ace, then Bice and now Gill-Roy's, along with Blue Cross Insurance, Jim & Donna's Flower Shop and others. The building saw its last use as a supermarket in the late 1990s and is, below, now the Victory Christian Center.

1506 West High Street. – The building was originally built in the 1960s as a Borden's Dairy Store when Chip-A-Waters Park opened across the street. The location soon became Tuma's Party Store, above, then Tuma's Country Store, then Tuma's Country Gourmet as the Tuma family turned the same expertise in food and it's preparation that made The Embers famous statewide to retailing fine meats and gourmet foods. In 2005, the business was sold to a group who phased out gourmet foods to turn the store into a standard convenience store, a move met with violent opposition that caused BD Party Store to close within a year. The store re-opened as Country Vineyard in 2008 and recently closed, with the owner opening a liquor store elsewhere. In August 2010, 1506 became the home of Tavola GiGi's, below, a new Italian restaurant that outgrew its South Mission location in less than a year.

114 South Bradley Street – The Clark Family Funeral Chapel is the newest of Mt. Pleasant's funeral establishments offering the full range of funeral services. The funeral chapel was built by Dane and Jane Clark in 1998 just south of the west end of Broadway Street.

440 South Bradley – Mt. Pleasant West Intermediate School, above, was built in the mid-1960s, after a ceiling collapse at the Mt. Pleasant Junior High School at 300 South Fancher Street indicated an eroding of the integrity of that 58 year-old building. West Intermediate serves 551 students at the 7th (256 students) and 8th grade (295 students) level with 35 full-time teachers in the 2010-2011 school year.

210 West Pickard – During the Great Depression, the Mt. Pleasant sugar beet processing plant was running three shifts and was welcome employment, albeit seasonal. The second shift at the Michigan Sugar Mt. Pleasant plant, in this undated 1930s photo, above, included: Lawrence Recker, Clarence Feltman, Marvin Hake, Ross Lindy, H. C. Walderf and Chester Davis. The plant produced an average of 233,000 bags of sugar in the seven years from 1935 to 1942. Below, Howard Sweet worked as a driver for the company after having been employed for several years by Renwick Elevator downtown.

210 West Pickard (continued) – Shrinking crops and yo-yoing prices caused Columbia to go bankrupt in 1931. In 1932, the Isabella Sugar Company was formed and the plant reopened and operated until 1942. In 1943, the sugar beet crop was so low no beets were processed in Mt. Pleasant. The plant opened again in 1944, but Mt. Pleasant area growers were no longer into sugar beets. The 1947 production was only 61,327 bags of sugar and the factory closed for the last time. In 1948, the plant sold to Michigan Sugar again, the equipment was sent to other plants. The building was abandoned for many years, owned for a time by Mt. Pleasant entrepreneur Gary Moore, before Chippewa Beverage Company bought the property, razed the building and built modern offices, below, in 1982, still operating at that address in 2010.

The West Pickard Street Bridge - After a major reconfiguration to accommodate a widened Pickard Street Bridge, renamed the Arnold and Margaret Sowmick Bridge in honor of a past Chippewa Indian tribal chief. The bridge officially opened November 19, 1979, in ceremonies presided by, left to right: City Manager Bill Barrons, Mayor Sibyl Ellis, Director of Public Works Robert Whitehead, D & L Contracting, Inc. John Cooley and the Michigan Highway Department's Larry Vernon.

300-700 West Pickard – Roosevelt Refinery, above, built in late 1928 and early 1929, alongside the railhead at Mt. Pleasant, was the deciding factor in bringing oil production from central Michigan oilfields to the community and establishing the community as the "Oil Capital of Michigan", which is the name of the next chapter.

300-700 West Pickard (continued) – Along the railroad tracks on West Pickard in the 1930s, the view above shows the remains of one of several fires that plagued the refinery in its half century history. The refinery, Roosevelt, then Leonard, then Total at Mt. Pleasant was phased out in the mid-1970s. The entire property is owned by McGuirk Sand and Gravel who, besides their own operations, are landlords of the old office building, below right, and the commercial development below, which includes the Mt. Pleasant Brewing Company, Advanced Detailing, , Absolute Granite, United Apartments, Modernistic, Paul's of Mt. Pleasant, and Howe's Alignment and Brakes.

711 West Pickard – Built in 1909 as the Transport Truck Company, which operated until 1921 at this location, producing truck, taxicabs and fire trucks, the building became American Enameled Products in 1926, center.

Ferro Stamping Company manufactured automobile parts here beginning in 1937 and tank parts during World War II before returning to car parts after the war. The plant closed in the early 1980s and is now the Commerce Center, below, housing among others, the Mt. Pleasant Morning Sun newspaper in 2010.

401 North Harris Street - This 1940s personal snapshot of Lynda and Brenda Utterback, in the front yard of the Kenneth "Red" Utterback home at 1012 Pennsylvania Street, is a rare glimpse of the West Side Church at the northwest corner of Pennsylvania and Harris streets, of which there seems little surviving record. The author's dimming memory recalls that the church may have been Methodist in denomination and could have been a survivor of the Bradley Mission school congregation because of its proximity just south of the Mt. Pleasant Indian Industrial School, next chapter. Robert Matthews was the minister. At any rate, there was a branch of the Mt. Pleasant Library in the basement open a couple days a week, a favorite haunt of the author as a youth. The building was torn down in the early 1950s and the site is now a private residence, below. "Red" Utterback, a popular and respected oilfield welder for 70 years, died at age 91 in February 2008.

CHAPTER 12:MAGNIFICENT COMEBACK ON WEST BROADWAY –

(With deepest gratitude to Mt. Pleasant's Bob Banta for the loan of his photos of the work in progress.)

320 West Broadway in 1906, the area later to be occupied by the Borden Milk Condensery, was the site of National Body and Box Company and the J.F. Butcher Company. Note the Harris Milling Company in the background upper left.

The Borden Company determined that they would need the production from 1,000 cows to warrant opening a milk condensery in Mt. Pleasant. A survey of the area in a ten mile radius of Mt. Pleasant found pledged production from more than 2,000 cows. Michigan Condensed Milk Factory acquired the site from the Ann Arbor Railroad with a 99-year lease, built the plant in 1908, and assigned ownership to the Borden family.

320 West Broadway (continued) -opened in 1908, above, and saw the staff of the new factory line up for an "opening day" photo, below, on the yet unpaved Broadway Street.

The Condensery, with its majestic chimney and water tower, soon became the ideal background for business and private portraits, like the folks above showing off their new cars.

Above, Bill Swanson and his mule team-drawn sled, made a 1908 winter milk delivery to the thriving plant.

Above, the Borden plant smokestack gets a refurbishing.
Below, when renovation began, the smokestack and water tank was deemed too far gone to reclaim and was felled.

Above, seen from the cupola of the Isabella County courthouse at 200 North Main, the Borden building and Harris Mill serve as backdrop for the stately pines on the courthouse lawn as well as the very busy Merritt Oil Company gasoline filling station, lower right.

Below, a 1950s view of the Borden plant across the Chippewa River from the west end of Island Park, just downriver from the Oak Street Bridge, a favorite "duck-feeding spot for generations.

320 West Broadway (continued) was alive for more than five decades with milk deliveries on conveyances ranging from horse and wagon to dairy trucks for Borden's Eagle Brand Sweetened Cream

The Creamery closed in 1960 and lay vacant until 1965 when Burton Bader bought it for $12,500 to use the property as a farm seed and fertilizer storage facility. Over the next 45 years, fifteen attempts were made to rehabilitate the building including: a community center; Department of Social Services offices; leasing to Sweeney Seed *Company* from 1980-1982; investigation of the site for Public Safety, City Hall office and Veterans Memorial Library by the City of Mt. Pleasant; an urban mall; Mid Michigan Community College campus; office condominiums; an arts and crafts arcade; multi-family housing units; a new Post Office; demolition; Social Security Administration building; Arts Campus for the Performing Arts; and low to moderate-income housing. All plans failed for financial or environmental reasons.

Finally, in 2003, Midland developer J. E. Johnson proposed a suitable development plan with the City of Mt. Pleasant involving renovation of the building, City Hall occupancy and further development of condominium housing on adjacent property to the west. In November, 2005, voters approved the sale of the City Hall property at 400 North Main, a critical element to the plan. Fierce debate and public outcry ensued but fortunately the enlightened City Commission hung tough for the worthiness of the project. With a variety of funding, including

Michigan Brownfield grants, Michigan Historical Department and Department of Natural Resources permits, renovation and restoration work began on the Borden building in 2007.

The West Broadway Street primary business entrance to the Borden Condensery is shown above in 1931, on the left of the forefront segment of the building, a portion of the conveyor run for return of the emptied and sanitized milk cans can be seen faintly, angling downward for easy movement and retrieval. Older locals will recall the hot sliding cans as bucking bronco substitutes, a dangerous practice and experience not shared or encouraged with younger generations.

During renovation, below, the Broadway entrance to the building was the most efficient for accessing what became the second floor of the City Hall offices.

While the water tower and the smokestack were determined to be dangerously beyond saving and had to be dropped before the main restoration work began, see previous pages. The eight decorative cupolas lining the Borden building roof were removed, reconstructed with great care to attend to detail in maintaining the integrity of the original construction, and returned to the roof as the crown jewels of the renovation.

The newly constructed upper floor of the Borden building was transformed into offices of the City Clerk, Cashier, City Manager and other departments.

More Borden renovation magic resulted in the spacious City Commission chamber at the east end of the lower floor of the building.

Work was completed and office move-in began - In the lower left corner above is a terraced walkway to West Broadway. This walkway angles southeast across the face of the "Borden Hill", site of many generations of town kid's sledding and sliding, left. City offices opened at 320 West Broadway in October, 2008.

The Oak Street Bridge behind the new City Hall began life as a wooden bridge built as south entrance to make Island Park easily available to visitors arriving in Mt. Pleasant by train at the Ann Arbor Railroad Broadway depot. The bridge served both pedestrian and limited vehicle traffic for several years before it collapsed under the weight of heavy equipment about 1913, below.

The Oak Street Bridge (continued) - When rebuilt, it continued as vehicle and pedestrian traffic until finally blocked by cement stanchions to restrict its use to pedestrians only for nearly six decades. In 1915, a cement arch bridge was built at the Main Street entrance to Island Park and the almost new, since 1910, steel truss bridge was moved to replace the wooden Oak Street Bridge. One of the last metal truss bridges remaining in mid-Michigan, the Oak Street Bridge was refurbished in 2010, below, after the conversion of the Borden Building to house Mt. Pleasant City Hall as it brought increased traffic to the area and underlined the need for bridge repair.

CHAPTER 11: MT. PLEASANT UNITED STATES INDIAN INDUSTRIAL SCHOOLS

The 1890-91 session of the United States Congress saw Congressman Aaron T. Bliss of Saginaw, later to be governor of Michigan, gain passage of a bill providing for the establishment and construction of Indian Industrial Schools in Wisconsin, Michigan, and Minnesota designed after the plan of the Indian school in Carlisle, Pennsylvania. The bill further stipulated that the buildings for the state of Michigan should be in the county of Isabella. Michigan Historical Marker #574 was mounted on the former Main Building front wall in 1987, above.

Construction of the Mt. Pleasant Industrial Schools began in 1892,
carved from the woods of northwestern Mt. Pleasant (*center left and opening page*). Above, looking east over Crawford Road, the foundation is about to be laid for the Boys Dormitory.

The following narrative is taken directly from Isaac A. Fancher's 1911 *Past and Present of Isabella County* book:

US INDIAN INDUSTRIAL SCHOOLS

"One of the institutions of interest to which all residents of Mt. Pleasant direct the attention of visitors is the United States Indian Industrial Schools. These schools are situated just outside the city limits on the northwest, being one mile from the business center of the city. The land upon which these schools are located was formerly known as the "Old Mission farm" and the "Mowry tract" and was selected by the United States government in 1891 as a location for these schools. There were 200 acres of land in these tracts, then valued at $8,400, of which amount the United States paid $5,000, and the citizens of this city contributed the balance that being used as an inducement toward securing the location of the schools at this point."

"The lands upon which the schools stand was formerly granted to the M.E. *(Methodist Episcopal – ed.)* church, for educational purposes being transferred by them to other parties, and finally repurchased by the government, as noted above. This tract includes the old reservation burying ground, and has been improved until today it is considered one of the finest farms to be found in this city."

"The corner stone for the main building was laid October 12, 1892, and the building was finished and occupied by the school on June 30, 1893. Since that time *(1892 to 1906 – ed.)* the schools have been gradually enlarged until the recent buildings consist of a Boys' Dormitory, a Girls' Dormitory, the Dining Hall, which building contains a large dining room with a seating capacity of 350, the kitchen and the bakery; the Steam Laundry, which is thoroughly equipped with all modern conveniences; the Hospital containing two wards and a dispensary, where the sick report each morning for treatment; the School House, which contains eight good-sized class rooms and a large chapel seated with opera chairs; the Power House, shops and barns and other out buildings. These buildings are all steam heated and lighted with electricity."

The Hospital

"The class room work is being carried on by a corps of six teachers, the pupils being taught through the eighth grade in their studies. Great stress is laid upon the industrial side of the schools and the different departments

Domestic Science Building

are all under competent heads, the manner in which the farm is handled, the out-buildings kept, and the character of the articles manufactured showing that thoroughness is one of the requisites which are carefully looked after."

"The girls are taught how to do all kinds of general house- work, such as cooking and dining room work laundry work, housekeeping, sewing and the elementary principles in caring for the sick.

"A Domestic Science class, composed of eight of the larger girls, is provided to train the girls in doing fancy cooking, such as pastry and cake making. A special kitchen and dining room is furnished this class and it is their duty to provide special meals, twice a day for eight, this for the purpose of training them in cooking and serving meals for small families."

The Cooking Class

"The boys have the following trades and occupations which they may learn by doing the practical work: farming,

tailoring, baking, carpentering, engineering, gardening, shoe and harness making and blacksmithing."

"A band consisting of 45 pieces has been organized among the boys and there are few like organizations that can furnish better music. An orchestra composed of both boys and girls, furnish music for all special occasions besides frequent engagements in Mt. Pleasant."

"The attendance at these schools at the present time is a trifle less than four hundred and one of the most interesting yet useful, of their teaching is the fire drill. At a moment's notice, and without any previous warning, the children march out of the building in a very orderly manner, these drills being frequent enough to ensure good results should necessity demand their use. The larger boys of the schools are formed into fire companies, they responding instantly to a fire alarm, no matter what work they may then be engaged."

"There are over 300 students at the school. Quite a number of them have graduated and are in the government employ".

"Knowing the tribal life of the Indian, one is surprised to see how soon they change to a large extent from their roving life to one of industry and good husbandry (farming). In their school all the common branches are taught, besides which they have domestic science and manual training. Many of them have good voices and are quite proficient in music. The

school supports a good brass band and they play baseball and football with proficiency." The Mt. Pleasant Indian Industrial School operated until 1934, when the land was turned over to the state of Michigan, which converted its use to the Mt. Pleasant branch of the Michigan Home and Training Schools, institutions for the mentally challenged.

The hospital on the grounds continued to function as Mt. Pleasant's hospital, above, until the Central Michigan Community Hospital was completed on Brown Street in 1946.

Reports of the Mt. Pleasant Industrial School experience vary from discontent to gratitude for a steady environment with regular meals, board, and vocational training. In 1938, more than 600 Chippewa alumni of the school held a powwow there to celebrate their years at the school.

The Mt. Pleasant Center grounds, in the northwest corner of the City of Mt. Pleasant, closed in October, 2009, and remains in a "much-rumored, but no concrete announced plan" limbo in late 2010.

CHAPTER 13; "BURNIE" BONNELL'S HISTORICAL REMEMBERANCES

NOTE: For many years, readers of the Mt. Pleasant Morning Sun newspaper have enjoyed the homespun writings of Auburna "Burnie" Bonnell, teacher, businesswoman and artist whose columns about Mt. Pleasant life. I am pleased to be able to share some of Burnie's writings, edited with permission (punctuated by photos from my own collection and the Norman X. Lyon Photo Collection of the Clarke Historical Library CMU Mt. Pleasant campus) especially for this publication. - J.R.W.

Mt. Pleasant Historical Remembrances
By Auburna "Burnie" Bonnell
Mt. Pleasant freelance columnist

In 1946, I'd been teaching Homemaking at Suttons Bay when I met Charlie Parks, superintendent at Mt. Pleasant High, at a convention in Lansing. He asked me to stop and see him on my way home since he was losing his Home Economics teacher to marry Mt. Pleasant High's principal, Lewis Wendt. He offered me $2,250 for the year to change jobs. Well! That was $500 more than I was getting…big money in those days.

Of course I made the move, rooming with Floyd and Olive Armstrong in the beautiful home now the annual Christmas light display showplace of Dot and Jerry Sheahan at 321 North Kinney Boulevard, right, for $8 a week.

You know the house, where people come by the hundreds each year to see Jerry's handiwork at creating a holiday wonderland of lights and displays.

While here to sign the teaching contract, I slept at The Park Hotel, at the northwest corner Broadway at Main, owned by Bert Creed, the white three-story building just right of center, above. It was a sticky-hot day, and only Dutch doors allowed the air to circulate. There were no locks on the doors.

When I came to town, Lew Wendt was Mt. Pleasant High's principal and had married the Home Economics teacher I was replacing. Charles Parks was superintendent and there had been Mr. Ganiard and Mr. Caszett before my time. At Sacred Heart Monsignor Edward N. Alt and Father Leo Fahrqueson are well remembered as active religious leaders.

Several unmarried young teachers gathered for breakfast at Alswede's restaurant, run by Radcliff and Wilma Sisk, southwest corner of Broadway and Mission. Sometimes we ate at Chris Moutsatson's Olympia on Broadway or at Newton's on campus. Where the now vacant Sweet Onion building stands at the northeast corner of Mission and Broadway, there was a two story brick home and the grocery business of Ellis and Pauline Howard. It was called Polly's market and opened into a regular farm and produce open air area, where fresh watermelons from Texas and other rare items were available.

My first impression of Mt. Pleasant was that it was flat as a pancake and lacked the hills, lakes with white birches, silhouetted like Traverse City, my hometown.

I won't be here long!" I said to myself.

Little did I dream that my home economics department head, Freddie Simonds, whose husband Lloyd's family ran the Simonds Grocery where Norm's Flower Petal sits now at 201 East Broadway, had other plans. She introduced me to a handsome, just back from the war, young man named Ed Bonnell Jr., who lost no time signing me up for dates, including a wedding 11 months later! We observed our 62nd anniversary before he passed, in 2009, at age 95!

So here I am, thoroughly in love with Mt. Pleasant and feeling like quite a real pioneer vastly interested in the startling changes I've witnessed.

On Broadway just off Mission, near Murray and Company wholesaler's big building, originally J.F. Battle Motor Sales, then Smale Chevrolet, and finally Archey Brothers Motor Sales,was Russ Alswede's Grocery.

Alva Gibson and Bernadine Johnson in the store that was originally Alswede's Grocery at 724 East Broadway.

As a newlywed living right across the street, I took my grocery list to Russ who cordially greeted customers and each item I asked for he'd pick off the shelves and lay it on the counter. It took a long pole to hook down a large box of cereal; sometimes a ladder reached high items. When finished Russ added up what I owed with pencil on a brown paper sack-by today's standard, very little!

The A & W Root Beer Drive-In, at 600 North Mission, was a favorite haunt for our family! Evenings we'd pile our four little children age 4, 5 6 and 7 into the car for what we called a "pajama ride" because they were bathed and in their pj's. A & W served delicious 10 cent root beer in heavy frosted glass mugs, with miniature mugs for the youngsters for a nickel.

Later at that location, under the ownership of Bill and Eva Mourtzouhos, later owners of the Downtown Restaurant, introduced the community to "broasted chicken". Now it is the home of Central Plumbing.

For ice cream treats everybody stopped at Mission Street McFarlane's Dairy Bar, formerly Brainerd's. They made awesome malts with an egg in them! Probably 15 cents for a large malt. They also delivered milk house to house throughout the county.

Off limits to teachers were the Flamingo at 223 South Main and the Moose Club upstairs, now The Bird, Martha Claus' M and M Bar, the dark and enticing Bennett Bar, the Bennett Hotel location is now Isabella Bank's main Mt. Pleasant operation, the Main Bar and the Cabin. But now and then a group of us, male and female, did meet for fish and a beer under cover of darkness at The Flamingo Bar, now The Bird.

The Blackstone Restaurant and Bar was where Allied Hearing is now located at 112 South Main, right, considered very elegant. I hear they served the best hamburgers in town!

I bought dry goods at Ed Conrick's Dry Goods and Apparel, now Total Eclipse Hair Design, under the helpful eye of clerk Louise Schubaugh, that paragon of courteous sales lady ship. We had charge accounts at Oren's, Marianne Fashion Center, owned by Lois Schlemmer, and Gittleman's. McKnight and Duhamel did a nice clothing business at Ace of Diamond's location.

Jack Beatty and Frank White had bought out Lewis' Men's store and it was renamed Beatty & White, later to become The Gentry owned by Bruce Barnum; Ken Paullin had Ken's Men's Shoppe. Ray Boulton, N.D. Gover and J.C. Penney's were downtown for men, also.

About 1920, Ed Bonnell Sr. and Ed Bixby Sr. bought Herb Foster's Hardware, Furniture and Funeral business, naming it Mt. Pleasant Hardware and Furniture Co., on the southwest corner of Main and Broadway. Boulton's Clothing was next door south, then Butts Drugs, then Sweeney's Grocery, with Sweeney's Seed almost directly behind at 110 South Washington, all on the west side of the 100 block Main Street.

At the northwest corner of Michigan and Main two gourmet shops thrived. Dondero's at 130 South Main, offered liquors and a confectionery of delicious candies, tons of "penny candy" and nuts. The store later became Wakefield's, Sisters 3, and Off Broadway, both women's fashion clothing stores. Next door to the

north, at 128 South Main, Spagunolo's, or "Spag's" was run Frank
and Virginia Spagnuolo, who lived upstairs at 1281/2 South Main
and sold meats and foodstuffs. Later the store was renamed Bills
Party Store. Ultimately both that store and the Dondero location to
the south were absorbed into the Brass Café, now downtown Mt.
Pleasant's most elegant eatery.

Joe Breidenstein owned a Kroger store at 111 South Main,
later to be Murphy's dime store. Upstairs was the Chippewa Lanes
bowling alley, later to become the corporate homes of Giant Super
Markets and Giantway Department Stores. Keenans and Johnsons
also had meat markets. "Honey's Hunk and Chunk" Grocery and
Meats, on Mission, now Dominos Pizza, was owned by friendly
big Dutch Honeywell who slaughtered his own beef and hogs and
featured fresh cuts every day. Dutch also sold my children penny
candies. "Ten candies for 10 cents!" exclaims my daughter, then
within walking distance of the store.

Sammy Pisho's dad sold delicious Coney-Island hot dogs at
the Minute Lunch on
North Main for 5 cents
each.

Kid's clothing
came from
the New Yorker owned
by Les Carr, and now
son Jack Carr, still
doing business in the
same location in the
100 block of South
Main Street right.

The New Yorker is the longest continuing downtown
enterprise operating in the same location by the same family since
1940s opening.

Hal and Gladys Wood's Tots 'n Teens Shop was first on
South College Street, then in the 100 block of East Broadway
Street. Shoes were sold by Johnson's on South Main, Dittman's,
and later at Lloyd's Footwear, on the northeast corner of Main and
Broadway. Bob Shackleford guided Oren's Department Store's
fine shoe department. On that corner's southeast, you could
indulge in a big hot fudge sundae at Smith's Drug Store. The Ward

Theater building was across Main Street and still is, having housed several churches; presently the Young Church.

Harris Furniture became Red Wood's Household and then became Household Furniture, having moved from a South Main location in the old firehouse across from the Ward Theater to the southeast corner of Broadway at Franklin Street owned first by Duane Gray and now by his son Mike.

Breidenstein and Kane handled hardware and furniture on Broadway, where Art Reach is now located. Out on Mission Street, Elmore's did their share, too, in carpet, appliances and furniture, where Jack Welch and Stan Elmore were the mainstays. Englishman Bill Davidge sold fine furniture on Michigan Street then built Superior Furniture 4 miles north of Mt. Pleasant on Mission road. He'd built it to become a motel, but when his health failed, sold it to my husband, Ed Bonnell Junior, in 1956. Ed had worked for years with his Dad, Ed Senior, downtown. Now he had a business of his own and for the next several decades I and the four children all had a part and learned the business.

The *Enterprise* newspaper became the *Isabella County Times*. John Doughty, Webb McCall, Norm Lyon were early editors. The newspaper's name changed from the *Times News,* the *Daily Times News,* and finally to the *Morning Sun.* All these changes encompassed a few mergers along the way.

Norman X. Lyon , he had no middle name so always used the "X" as a middle initial, was alternately editor of the daily paper and edited the *Michigan Oil and Gas News magazine*, only one of its kind in the U. S. of A. He was a clever writer, excellent speaker, a leader well known to all, with a wild sense of humor.

Lynn Leet, started the Buyer's Guide at 200 East Broadway, later moving the operation, basically a mimeograph machine, to the front porch of his home on Pine Street at the east downtown terminus of Michigan Avenue. Later the Buyer's Guide, now with a press, moved to the former Albar Nash Motors Sales building in the 100 block of South Washington Street. Still later, the Buyers Guide expanded by building a modern two-story building facing East Michigan Street, forming an "L" around Sheppard's Pure Oil filling station, now Curt's Service Center. The Buyer's Guide ultimately merged with the Morning Sun parent company, which has changed ownership and names a number of times.

In 1946, a new car cost $1,200. A new house was $6,000. Gas was 15 cents a gallon and the Dow Jones average was 177. Silly putty, Frisbees, microwave ovens and long playing records were invented. In that year, Steven Speilberg, Johnny Bench, Farrah Fawcett and Arnold Swartzenegger were born. Harry Truman was president with no vice president. Ronald Coleman won best actor award for "Double Life"; Loretta Young for "The Farmer's Daughter". Top songs were "Chi-Baba, Chi-Baba", "Tenderly", and "Almost Like Being In Love".

Joe Lewis KO'd Joe Walcott, "Jet Pilot" won the Kentucky Derby and New York won the World Series.

Lee, Theo and Echo Ward were brothers who managed the Ward Theater on South Main Street and Broadway Theater on East Broadway followed by Lee's son, Kent Ward. Some of you will remember that movie houses often offered vaudeville acts live on  the stage, especially before Saturday's double feature. Our brother-in-law, Elwyn Merrill, was one of the hired organists at the Ward, while he was in high school and college. Of course popcorn and cokes were 5 cents. I bought a large sack of grapes for five or ten cents at the grocery store and ate them during the movies.

I swooned over Clark Gable, Betty Davis, and George Raft and copied Joan Crawford's hair-do. I wept with Joan Fontaine, Olivia DeHaviland and Franchot Tone. I thought Robert Taylor just a bit too pretty. But Nelson Eddy, Jeanette McDonald, Norma Shearer and Merle Oberon…on and on! Charles Laughton was part of my growing up. Yet I can't forget Rooney, Garland, Gaynor, Our Gang, George Stone, Billy Gilbert, Marie Dressler, Lew Ayres and Richard Arlen. QUIT ALREADY, Burnie! With Eddie Robinson, Joel MacRae and Shirley Temple! Well, and Jean Harlow, Greer Garson, Victor McLaughlin and Mae West.

Real Estate was sold by Henry Rothlisberger, Charles Durfee, John Brien, Ann Gorthy, Don Stinson and others. A shave and haircut while you caught up on all the news were enjoyable at Al Schlemmer's, Sid Struble's, Bob Cook's and Art Fountain's barber shops. Insurance needs were enthusiastically met by "Tip" Carnahan, Walt Russell, Ralph and Bob Crapo, Bernie Wyman, Ed Bross and Ed Corey, Roy Leonard and Arlie Osborn. Arlie Osborn also coached the state championship high school basketball team of 1932 and 33 – something not won since! Ed Bonnell was the last living member of that team.

In 1946, when I arrived here, Mt. Pleasant was still thriving as "The Oil Capital of Michigan".

While the rest of the country was reeling under the Great Depression of 1929, the Mt. Pleasant oil field, discovered in 1928, shielded the town from the worst of the financial devastation suffered by much of our nation. Mt. Pleasant was fortunate to be spared from the Great Depression.

Jack Westbrook, retired editor of Michigan Oil and Gas, in his 2006 book *Michigan Oil and Gas,* included a picture of a hearse bearing an effigy of "Old Man Depression" leading the Mt. Pleasant parade opening the 1935 Michigan Oil and Gas Exposition, which drew  more than 20,000 visitors to our Island Park.

The effigy was thrown in the Chippewa River from the East Broadway bridge (the longest cement span bridge in Michigan when it was built at the turn of the 20th Century).

Active pioneers of our oil and gas industry were Walter McClanahan, whose wife died in a tragic explosion of a celebrated first well, I.W. (Bucky) Hartman, Earl Hartman, Norm Lyon, D.F. Jones - Olga Denison's father, G. Rollie Denison, Charles Daugherty - Betty Huber's father and Jack Long. Many others were part of this major local industry –James Leonard, Walter Leonard, Bob Tope, Noah Andrews -Coal miner to rotary driller, "Tip" Carnahan - Sally Weisenburger's father), Ollie Irwin, Walter Russell, Dean Eckersley, and Carl Wender.

Many of these citizens were civic leaders.

Mt. Pleasant's automobile sales industry was thriving. Hibbered-Thompkins sold Chrysler and Dodges. Van Grimley was service manager for John Battle's Buick, Cadillac and Chevy sales. My husband bought a brand new blue Nash (to "match my eyes!" he said) from Al Albar to take on our honeymoon to the U.P. Art Savage had the Oldsmobile Agency, later bought by Carl Archey. Lee Johnson sold Studebakers, which ultimately moved to Canada to produce refrigerators and stoves, and was scarcely heard of again.

Leo Beard represented Mercury, Lincoln, Lincoln Continental and the ill-fated Edsel at 107 East Illinois.

Krapohl Ford was on Court Street, displaced to East Pickard with the extension of Mosher Street to Washington. Naumes sold Hudson and Essex. Earl Hartman bought the Cadillac-Pontiac agency, as did Neil Sowle later, and now the business is Shaheen Motors in 2010.

Gorham Brothers Table Factory was on Oak Street. West from downtown on Broadway, where a special "mill run" was dug to use water power from the dammed up Chippewa River at the Millpond, Ed Harris milled the famous FAMO pancake flour, and Ken Elliott's floral business flourished then as now with the greenhouse at 800-804 West Broadway, just west of the entrance to Riverside Cemetery.. Mr. and Mrs. Les Adams' floral and gift shop was on the east side of south Mission Street, where the Speedway filling station and convenience store is now located.

One of the most charming sights in Mt. Pleasant is Fancher Elementary School, a stonecutter's showpiece, built in 1932 by the father and grandfather of Arlene Smith. Marion Clare Stahl and

VanDorn Stahl cut those field stones, an astounding feat! Franklin Roosevelt's WPA workers did the actual construction of Fancher Elementary. Three houses had to be removed in the 800 block of South Kinney Boulevard, at High Street, to make way for the most modern school of its kind in the state.

Babies were delivered at Cummins Nursing Home and Hospital, and at Dr. Bronstetter's Hospital. Dr. Northway had a hospital at 103½ South Main Street, above the Exchange Savings Bank. These were years before Central Michigan Community Hospital became a reality.

Dr. Charles Baskerville's family practice was housed on the northeast corner of Michigan at College Avenue, later on Court Street. Dr. Wes McGinnis and Dr. Clifford Anderson and Dr. C.B. Wood, and I remember a Dr. Burch, administered to the medical needs of the community. Midwife Lena Cummins delivered hundreds of babies.

Russ Stinson owned a funeral home at 330 College (now University) Avenue. Three other Stinson brothers-Art, Harold and Don had other careers. Stinson became Stinson-Helms and finally, in 1973, was bought by long-time employee Harry Helms and his wife Alice. When Harry Helms passed away in 1980, his wife Alice continued operation of the funeral home until her retirement in 2010, when she sold the funeral home to long time employee, Sherman Rowley and his wife Shirley.

The other funeral home in town was J.J. Rush Funeral Home at 503 East Broadway. The Fancher and Broadway intersection was so prone to automobile mishaps that Joe Rush used to keep a broom and dustpan by the door to sweep up head and tail light glass after the wreckers hauled the cars away. The Rush Funeral Home became the Lux Funeral Home, owned by Charles Lux, Senior, and now his son Charlie Junior, who moved the business to 2300 Lincoln Road in 2008.

If you needed a doctor an appointment or house call were in order with veteran doctors Harrigan, Hersee, Lionel Davis, LeRoy Juhnke, Don Nagler, Andy Bedo, Leo Wickert and John Wood. Early MDSs included R. Burch, C.B. Wood, Phil Johnson, Drs. Crapo and Gardiner, Ray Chamberlain and doctors Hyslop and Brondstetter. Dear, gentle Dr. Mary Maxwell could give a heavenly back rub, head adjustment and hear your troubles for $4.

Dental experts included Drs. Howard Woodruff and "Doc" Sweeney, Drs. Slaughter and Pullen, for whom Pullen School, right, was named) and Vince Brown.

Prescriptions were filled at Clabeusch Drugs, with a lunch counter, where Simply Engraving operates today, Smith's Mt. Pleasant Drugs, Johnson's Rexall, now Headliners, and Butt's Drug Store.

"One piece or a carload" was the slogan of Mr. Pleasant Lumber, owned by William Hood the first. Homes could be built for five to ten thousand dollars. Ed finished off an attic bedroom for our boys with lumber costing less than $200. Cousins to William, Bert Hood and his sons, Bob and Herb, competed at Hood Lumber Company.

Hardware stores included Hafer's, Kirky Electric, Gambles, Ace and Richmond & Shangle. Builders of homes were Pratt & Howe, Lloyd Cole, Lee Jones, Charles Post, Mt. Pleasant Lumber, Hood Lumber, Clarence Smalley and others. I enjoyed measuring for draperies in homes Smalley built because windows were never "off" even a 32nd of an inch. You could count on it!

Special services and merchandise were provided by Archey Sporting Goods, Gover's Campus Store, Tice Ice, The Coldwater Lake Inn, Sweeney Seeds and Plants, Mike Murphy's Beauty School, Harold Bentley at the Pickwick Office Supply, Kinney's Wholesale, Murray Candy and Cigarettes, Gene Knight at American Cleaners, Maxim Cleaners, Charlie Craft's Woodworking, Roy Houghtaling's Picture Framing, Del Conkright's Photo, Harry Francisco Photo and Collins Photo Studio.

An exquisite little shop called Bishop's Boutique on the northwest corner of Broadway and Franklin sold ladies' negligees, fine gloves, linens and laces. Later the building, at 215 East Broadway, housed the Minute Lunch, when it was displaced by the demolition of all buildings from Broadway to the 200 block of North Main, the Central Inn, H. & R. Block, William J. Wood Associates Printing, and presently the American Red Cross is located there, across from Household Furniture.

A roller rink filled an old wooden building on South Mission at Gaylord Street, run by another Davis family.

Chippewa Bowling Lanes, upstairs at 110½ South Main, thrived under friendly Art Periard. Bowl three strikes in a row;

he'd give you a turkey for thanksgiving. I know because I won one! Jewelers were George Foland, Dave Young, Thompson Jewelers (Ted Foley), and Voisin's. Eyes were tested and glasses fitted by Drs. George Brown, Bill Hersee, Fred Schall, with Dr. Fred Anderson coming later.

Beauty shops were kept busy back-combing intricate hairstyles. When an operator knew me so well that she could chat with a salesman while doing my hair, I'd find another shop where I'd be paid more courteous attention. Notable was Lenore Conkright. She set the pace. Her skill and enthusiasm brought customers. She hired good helpers and often helped them establish a shop of their own. Operators I remember include Guylyn King, Chris Fairbanks, Dorothy Horgan, Gladys Sponseller and the great LENORE.

Downtown on the corners banks flourished under Chet Richie at Exchange Savings Bank, Bill Anderson and Joe Hauck. Evan Weidman was a famous citizen and president of Isabella Bank, before John Benford and Elmer Graham.

Lee Browning, Gerald Cotter, M. B. Decker, George Duzenbury, Stephen Fox, Byron Gallagher, Allen Lampman, and James MacNamara, Russ Otterbine, James Ryan, Joseph Schnitzer and Barnie Wendrow, many of whom became judges at some time in their legal careers, also had law offices in town.

Virgil, Jean, and Burke McClintic practiced law from a stately old home at 500 South Main Street, left.

In the 60s Bill Kelly, Chelsea Utterback, and Superintendent Russ LeCronier, along with many helpers, engineered the building of a new high school football stadium.

We in Central Michigan have much to be thankful for. Our weather is mostly safe and varied. Autumns are gorgeous. Shaded streets, lovely homes of every vintage, a fine university, great sorts and cultural opportunities, friendly people of widely colorful and diverse backgrounds offering expertise in nearly every area of life, outstanding civic leaders and philanthropists, citizens who champion vital causes...these are some of our pluses. We have the Chippewa River, the Mill Pond, Island Park and other parks to enjoy. We are proud of our golf pros – Kelly Robbins, Dan Pohl and Cindy Fig-Currier, our championship athletes and teams. The cost of living is moderate, shopping is great. We are enriched by the resources of Central Michigan University: libraries, and art programs. We owe much to our alert police force, our fire department, Hospice, 911 and our doctors, pharmacists, merchants, UPS and post office, Central Michigan Community Hospital, the Morey Cancer Treatment Center, and Central Michigan University's planned medical school.

Our Saginaw Chippewa Indian Tribe has generously turned the other cheek. They enrich and color our history with their arts and ceremonial dignity and are now helping build much needed youth facilities, and adding to the growth of our area with part of the proceeds from their gaming enterprises, which have made them Isabella County's largest employer. The story of our university and its leaders is so vast; it may wait for another to unveil its epoch (Jack R. Westbrook's 2007 photo history book *Central Michigan University* tells the story of the people for whom CMU buildings are named for academic reasons).

Notable Gardens and Gardeners

Adams' Flower and Gift Shop was on the east side of Mission at Michigan. At one time I picked and spray-painted exquisite baby cattails for Les Adams to use in arrangements...just for fun, as I was making winter bouquets those days myself. Mine also sold at Mt. Pleasant Furniture and Hardware downtown.

Dean and Lucille Snider had a greenhouse on South Mission Road. They gave many programs and demonstrations related to planting, flower arrangement and wedding preparation and tradition. Betty Horton nurtured an impressive flower border of spring tulips, crocus, hyacinth and begonias in her High Street yard. Lloyd and Freddie Simonds, on Fancher Street, favored a variety of lovely peonies, and gave starts to friends each year. A yard on West Broadway was aflame with big red poppies. I snapped pictures from which I have done several watercolor paintings. Elliott Greenhouse has operated at the East Broadway entrance to Riverside Cemetery (Mt. Pleasant's oldest) for decades.

The Walter Leonard home on the northeast corner of High and Fancher was always surrounded by picturesque and colorful gardens.

After Mt. Pleasant High School teacher and builder Lee Jones built the home at 1110 Kent Drive for the late Rollie and Olga Denison, right, Olga's "green thumb" became very apparent. "To me, gardening is like painting…on the landscape!" Olga said "When winter comes it erases the canvas and you start over again." Her yard was a true art form. Many a visitor has thrilled to the exquisite mixed gardens she visualized into  reality. Because when Olga looked out any one of many windows, she'd imagine what she'd like to see each season. Then she made it happen! The result was a constantly changing, artistically conceived feast of color, flower groups, shrubs and trees, statuary, rocks, art objects, homes and feed for birds, and rolling green lawns. Approaching the Denison home a figure of St. Frances of Assisi stood amid the plantings. A plaque read: "There is beauty in the sunlight and the soft blue heaven above. Oh! "The world is full of beauty when the heart is full of love."

I am reminded of another personal favorite: "The kiss of the sun for pardon, the song of the birds for mirth … One is nearer God's heart in a garden, than anywhere else on Earth!"

Belle's Hat Shop

Quaint and proper Belle LaForge whose hat shop at 205 East Broadway was the place to buy your Easter bonnet. Women not only wore hats in those days-they got very excited about them-the cloche, the stroller, the pill box, the tam, the picture hat, the alluring facial nets and veils, the turbans and helmets, straws, ribbons, felts, florals. One year I wore an upside down basket of pink roses, even though it was snowing Easter Sunday. A man in church told me how good it made him feel-seeing that hat! I guess it was a breath of spring after a long cold winter. Belle led the fashion parade with her outsized hats perched on upswept hair.

Each year we eagerly watched her shop window for the latest trends. Then we'd go in, be seated, and try on hat after hat 'til there was one we could not live without! Lucille Robinson became the hat shop's next owner.

Doctor Charles Mackenzie

No history of Mt. Pleasant would be complete without recalling a local citizen, who in his time probably did more for the greatness of our town than any other person. He was my friend and pastor Charles Mackenzie, a peppy, little Scotsman whose tenure of 30 years as minister of First United Methodist Church was unmatched.

His laughter rang through the halls of all the institutions he helped start. He went to Washington D.C. at his own expense and fought to get our hospital financed and built.

He was a caring friend and supporter of the Chippewa Indians, defending their rights, looking out for their welfare, helping them build churches and be recognized. An Indian School, where the State Home stood on West Pickard, educated Indian students. My husband remembered some of the fine Indian athletes he played basketball against!

Charles Mackenzie shepherded his flock in the old church on south Main Street, preaching every Sunday, visiting and counseling the sick and needy, working hard for all the organizations he was a member of serving on the city council, filling speaking engagements. When Methodists met for supper or song, he was there early in the basement of the church, setting up tables, unfolding chairs, complimenting the cooks, notably Helen (cook for Mt. Pleasant High School) and Arnold Koch (Mt. Pleasant High School Science Teacher and head of the high school's Audio-Visual Department), on delicious meals prepared with a minimum of poor equipment on the old stoves. He moved fast, always on the go. He once confided to me, "The only happiness I have ever known has come from service to others." Toward the end of his ministry here, he was packing them in to hear the wisdom, the hope and heart of his sermons.

He was instrumental in the establishment of Veterans Memorial Library.

He married and buried folks, baptized babies, ate heartily, and his laughter and humor were contagious, never hurtful.

When he retired in the 60s, Robert Smith came to replace him and build the new church. Mackenzie and his wife, Mae, moved to an apartment in Detroit. In my opinion this was just one more unselfish sacrifice this loving minister made realizing no doubt that his well known presence might overshadow the effectiveness of his young replacement that indeed had a hard act to follow! Charles and Mae accepted isolation and loneliness as a necessary gift to his successor.

He came back as guest preacher a few times, just as cordial and interested as ever! Just a few visited them in Detroit; a sad fact. I wish I'd had the realization of how overjoyed they were to see any friend, and gone to them! But I was too busy with babies and business. There was a lesson I did not learn.

Soon the beautiful old First United Methodist Church came tumbling down. It is still a source of sad amazement to me that the wonderful stained glass windows of all sizes and shapes, were smashed to the floor in the wrecking process. I salvaged a few pieces of the colored glass for Rose Wunderbaum Traines to use in sculptures. How dear those windows would be to us now, had we valued them and saved them.

Marie Richmond, and her Piano Songsters

L.D. Richmond represented Blue Cross and was the architect who designed a table which stands at the entrance of the Isabella County Court House. L.D. and wife, Marie had a big family (10 I believe). Marie had played for silent movies and once had her own dance band. For decades, happy, fun loving folk lucky enough to be able to carry a tune, gathered around Marie. Attorney Loren Gray is one such, a tenor. Whether she was playing at the Chieftain Hotel, the Holiday Inn Lounge, the Green Spot, for CMCH'S High Fever Follies, weddings at Sacred Heart, or the Doherty Hotel in Clare where Lucille Doherty requested her favorite, "San Francisco", and sang along.

Some of the regulars were Del Conkright, Anita Preston, Mary Jane Post, Chuck Lang, Shirley Bragg, Bobbie Lassiter, Jane Cascarelli, Joyce Pepperman, and Paul Jensen. Bill Stahl, a physical therapist and bartender at Jerry Sheahan's Green Spot sang a heartfelt rendition of "Danny boy". Marie loved to play St. Louis blues, Basin Street blues. The singers sometimes breakfasted together at her home in the early morning hours. She was always chipper and happy and so proud of her children and grandkids an unfailingly kind lady, full of fun.

One night a couple from Flint came to the Doherty Hotel. The man said, "We just got married. My wife likes to sing". They joined the group around Marie at the piano and sang until one in the morning on their wedding night. Marie autographed a songbook for them. Mike Cameron of Alma was ever part of the groups from the 60s to the 90s. Mt. Pleasant's Bob Klein, head wrapped in a towel (turban), sang a mean "The Sheik Of Araby"! John Warren of Clare performed on spoons and ashtrays. One night a fellow in a tux asked, "Would you mind if I played?" turned out he'd played with Liberace for 17 years in the 40s and 50s. He played a concert so great that A.J. Doherty broke out the house' best wine and waitresses finally shooed the gang out at 2 a.m. Rain or shine, blizzards and all, Marie Richmond was at a piano someplace, creating joy and fellowship for her songsters.

B.B.

Rowe Hall, above, was built in the mid-1950s at the extreme northeast corner of the Central Michigan College Campus, near the southeast corner of Mission and Bellows Streets. The College Elementary School, east wing of the building, burned after the school closed in 1969. Note two-lane Mission Street (US 127) just left of the east wing.

CHAPTER 14: FACES & PLACES - PAST & PRESENT

In 1938, the Mt. Pleasant Elks Lodge No. 12164 hosted 13 charter members of the local order in ceremonies observing the 29th anniversary of the organization in Mt. Pleasant. Above are eleven of the charter members who were present at the ceremonies. Left to right are: Front Row: Fred Klunzinger – Mt. Pleasant; H. W. "Bucky" Coddington – Mt. Pleasant: Frank Seibel - Grand Rapids; E. T. Cameron - Lansing; Ivan D. Wallington - Cleveland; and Chester Kellogg – Mt. Pleasant. Back Row: Harold Preston – Mt. Pleasant; Charles Carnahan – Mt. Pleasant; James Johnson – Mt. Pleasant; Bert Cook – Shepherd; Walter Russell – Mt. Pleasant; and Selb Adams - Shepherd. Charter members present but not pictured were: Mayor John Benford and J. F. McNutt, both of Mt. Pleasant.

Woodrow Eber found this skull while hiking his property in Chippewa Township in 1956. After a lot of speculation about dinosaurs and such, experts concluded it was probably a moose skull, which Woody kept at his home for many years.

City Manager Al Kronbach and Police Chief Vernel Davis present the new "NO TURNS" sign at Broadway and Main, above, in the early 1950s. Effectiveness of the effort is demonstrated below. By spring the no turns pylons had disappeared.

Police Chief Vernel Davis seemed to have a number of ideas for Mt. Pleasant traffic control in the 1950s. Davis, right above, implemented utilization of the three-wheeled "scooter" for more manuverable traffic control, being inspected here with Officers Fred Bell and Art Oles. The vehicle would suffer a irreparable mishap under officer Wayne Van Dyke years later.

Left, Davis showed off the new free-standing portable School Zone warning signs, furnished by Coca Cola, at the Mission and Andre Streets intersection, with Leo Beard's Phillips 66 filling station and sporting goods establishment. Beards, like Pete Millers at the other end of town on Mission, stayed open 24 hours a day during the opening weekends of trout season in the spring and deer season in the fall, rarities in the day.

Mt. Pleasant Police Chief Vernel Davis was also vigilant about the condition of cars on the road, as attested by the random safety inspection lines set up periodically throughout the city to check the condition of brakes and lights, above. Bicyclists were also also subject to safety inspection and licensing of their vehicular mode, below, with Charles Fitzpartick (center) getting his thumbs up and safety sticker.

City Attorney Edward N. Lynch, left above, had a six-member jury observe speed-time operation in November, 1956, as prelude to a jury trial in which a motorist had been tagged by Mt. Pleasant's new "semi-robot" cop and protested the ticket. Officer Maynard Pickens operated the machine for, left to right beyond Lynch: Officer Tom Martin, Defendant Gordon McKinnon, Attorney Ray D. Markel, Judge James E, Ryan, jurors – Kenneth Elliott, Jessie Haight, William Downey, Joy Allswede, Louise Bissett and Leona Quinlan, Attorney B. A. Wendrow and Police Chief Vernel Davis.

Down on Central's campus, officers come to the aid of an early version of the "smart car" owner outsmarted by pranksters who put the front wheels over a parking lot border log in the autumn of 1955.

Duncan McGregor, K. P. Wood and Gaylord Courter do kitchen duties to prepare 2,000 pancakes, 4,300 feet of sausage and 50 gallons of coffee at the 1956 Kiwanis Pancake Supper at Sacred Heart Church's downstairs parish hall. Below, a municipal street sweeper, driven by Lahdy Bailey, tipped over on Chippewa Street in July, 1956.

1956 Mt. Pleasant High School Future Farmers of America (FFA) officers, above, left to right Allan Block - President, Pat O'Brien – Treasurer, and Robert Neeland are shown with the high school's Vocation Education Director Richard Hickman. Below, in October 1956, the FFA helped collect grain and cash to send overseas during CROP Week. Right, Ray Hoyle, in charge of crop collections in Union Township, and Richard Hickman, left, outline collection plans with FFA volunteers. The volunteer group included: Roger Sheets, Alan Block, Rudy Block, Marvin Bellinger, Gary Dangler, Bob Downing, Larry Ervin, Denver Harless, Gary House, Sam Hart, Lisle Hunter, Larry Mead, Murray Morrison, Bob Neeland, Pat O'Brien, Dick Straka and Bill Thering.

306 East Andre was home to and the site of Pete Moutsatson's early 1950s drink stand. Pete (seated), following the family tradition of food service to the public, pours another round, above, for customers Gene Moutsatson and Marty Elliott. The Moutsatson boy's father, Jim, ran downtown eateries the Metropole at 208 East Broadway in the 1940s and '50s and the Elite at 110 South University in the 1960s.

Below, at the northeast corner of Main and Broadway, Junior Chamber of Commerce (Jaycee) Dean Eckersley receives a donation for an emergency polio fund from Mrs. Ed "Burnie" Bonnell in 1949.

Kiwanis Old Newsboys of the 1970s - Chief among Kiwanis fund-raisers, then and now, is the Old Newsboys Newspaper Sale, above in the 1970s, that takes place each holiday season. Ready to hit the bricks of a bygone era are, left to right: Ed Bakus. George Rouman, Ed Bonnell, -?, Richard Wysong, Charlie Cain, Don Gould, Van Grimley Woodrow Eber, Bob Gover, Dennis Marsh, Jerry Moravy, Lornie Hood, -?-. -?-, George Clapp, Dean Russell, Tom Peters, Howard R. "Doc" Woodruff, Raul Cole, Bill Kelly, Elmer Grahm, -?-, Arlie Osborn, Norman X. Lyon, and Earl Hartman.

Below – John Wezensky, Martin Trombley, Bill Cain and Arlie Osborn lend a hand fixing the Little League Baseball diamond at Pickens Field, just west of the Chippewa River Bridge on West Pickard Street.

Biography of a civic club: Mt. Pleasant Civitans – Civitans International is an association of community service clubs founded in 1917 to "build good citizenship by providing a volunteer organization of clubs dedicated to serving individual and community needs with an emphasis on helping people with developmental disabilities." The Mt. Pleasant Civitan Club was chartered March 23, 1959, with James R. "Red" McLean President. Above, at a 1965 installation of offices, are, left to right: Elton Watson, Don White, Harold Wallace (new President), Civitan District Governor Anson Hobbs, Warren Assman, Walt Utterback, Perry Blake, William J. Wood, Fred Cashen, and Gordon Gilray.

Civitans Bill Wood, Ken Schrock, Dick Bellinger, Elmer Flaugher and Al Roy (who donated the painting equipment) display some of the 30 bicycles rejuvenated and freshly painted by the club as Christmas presents to deserving local children.

Biography of a civic club: Mt. Pleasant Civitans (continued) – Mt. Pleasant Mayor Jackson K. Beatty, center, signs a proclamation designating the week beginning February 3, 1963, "Clergy Week" in the city, while Civitan President Gerald Cassel and Secretary Dale Jarrett look on.

The Mt. Pleasant Civitans operated for thirteen years, bringing the community the American version of the world famous Oberammergau Passion Play, helping out at the Special Olympics, refurbishing bicycles as Christmas presents for local children, and in general performing a number of community services. Like many organizations, the fiery enthusiasm of founding members faded and attrition by retirements, transfers and expirations, along with failure to attract new members and the Mt. Pleasant Home and Training School's change in client profile from developmentally disabled children to an institution for those with other, mostly adult, disabilities, led to the club's revoking their charter in 1982. Civitan International Louis Stevens, Vice President of Membership, awaits newcomers to perhaps form a new Mt. Pleasant Civitans Club.

Mt. Pleasant Rotary Club Old-Timers were honored at their Michigan Week Veteran's Day Luncheon in May, 1958. Seated are: Ed Bonnell Sr., Bob Kane, and Harry Gover. Standing are other 25 year Rotarians: Dale Richmond, Malcolm Wardrop, Hendrick Theunissen, N. D. Gover, Ray Monroe, John Benford Sr., Howard Renwick and Ralph Crapo.

Wesley Welsh, left with his signature tie he wore to do farm chores, purchased 60 acres on the corner of Pickard and Isabella roads in 1944, adjacent to the 2010 east Mt. Pleasant City Limits . He added another 20 acres to the west in 1947, near what in 2010 is Belmont Drive. Also in 1947, he sold the southeast of the property to Henry Magus for a Cities Service gasoline station, now the Mt. Pleasant Rental Center. Wesley operated a small dairy farm and sold eggs. In 1970, his widow sold the land to Mt. Pleasant Lumber Company, which became Erb Lumber and in 2010 is Mid-Michigan Health Care Park, Applebee's restaurant, and the Celebration Cinema movie theater complex.

Sam Marks, who died in June 16, 1990, one day after his 109th birthday was arguably the most active of senior citizens known to the author. Sam was the father of Eva Mourtzouhos, who with husband Bill owned the Chicken Shack on North Mission followed by the Downtown Restaurant until the 1980s. Born June 15, 1881, in Korfoula, Greece he married Chrisoula Gersios there. A veteran of the Greek Army, Sam came from Greece to Mt. Pleasant in 1952 with his wife, four daughters: Florence, Melle, Eva and Sandra, along with two sons: Milton and Ike, when Communists destroyed their native village. Sam's brother Ike was already in Mt. Pleasant and owned the Coffee Cup Restaurant at 123 North Main, later sold to Mark Achelles. Sam, below, with brother Ike, Eva and Melle Marks, worked with Ike for awhile before opening his own restaurant, the Minute Lunch, first on Court Street and finally at 305 East Broadway. Sam sold out in the late 1960s and the Minute Lunch moved to 215 East Broadway.

Young athletes of Mt. Pleasant Past – The Mt. Pleasant High School Cross Country team had five letter winners in 1949: Hudson Keenan, Joe Moose, Bill Coughlin, Don Durfee and Emmett Van Aucker.

Twelve years later, this baseball team celebrated a 4-3 win over Essexville- Hampton. Included in the picture are Lew Lawriski, with a fist of victory lifted in the center background, Mike York holding the four balls that sent him to first base, forcing the winning run, and the following team members, named in approximate left to right order according to the July 23, 1961, issue of the *Mt. Pleasant Daily Times-News*: Mike Funnell, Rick Elkins, Gil Maienknecht, Tom Sutton, Mike Goodwin, Bill Sutton, Glen Stiegemeier, Bob vonReichbauer, Mike Kostrzewa, Bob Servoss, Geof Elias, Jim Cooper, Jim Schall and Scott Voison.

The St. John's Episcopal Church Title VII Foodsite drew a record 65 people in April of 1976 for a nutritious meal, a salute to the Irish and music by the Kitchen Band, making their second anniversary performance, along with solos by Mt. Pleasant painter/guitarist Herb McBride.

It's not exactly a face, but this photo of one of the three Quonset-style houses that lined the north side of 1002 block of Bruce Street was too tempting not to be included. They stood into the 1960s.

321 North Kinney Street – The spirit of joyous Christmas home display is kept alive annually at the home of Gerald and Dorothy Sheahan, who for the past two decades have lavishly lit their home and property, inviting people to stroll and bring the kids to sit in the sleigh, marvel at the antimated figures and maybe even get a candy cane from a costumed elf or Mrs. Santa. The display, from Thanksgiving to New Years Day, draws visitors for miles. No "Bah, humbugs" at this address.

926 South Mission Street was the home of the Mt. Pleasant School System Central Kitchen, which doubled as a seasonal community canning center. Later the building would become the high school auto mechanics lab and in 2010 the adress belongs to the Mission Pharmacy shopping complex Left to right, Emma Kisch, Lucille Porter, Manager Lucille Moor and Gladys Heinlein prepared 392 pounds of turkey for students and teachers Christmas dinner in 1956.

Michigan Governor Kim Sigler was a frequent visitor to the Mt. Pleasant airport for annual Dawn Patrols, above, and Governor G. Mennen Williams always showed up for the Isabella County Youth and Farm Farm Fair.

319 South University – Important 2010 Change #1. Around 1890 a group of Mt. Pleasant citizens became interested in the Christian Science Church movement. They organized loosely and formally chartered on January 15, 1891, as the Mt. Pleasant Christian Science Church, meeting in various private homes. They then found that they needed a church building and they finally selected and purchased the home and site of the Richard Balmer home on lot 8 of Block 33 (319 South Church Street) on the 18th day of July, 1907.

The residence was remodeled. into a very convenient and spacious church, very prettily finished, and decorated with beautiful windows. On April 19, 1908, the church was dedicated.

In 1981, several art groups in Mt. Pleasant merged to create Art Reach of Mid Michigan and acquired the Christian Science Church building, which was transformed into an art center.

In 2000, Art Reach purchased a building at 111 East Broadway, which became the organization's office and gift shop.

In 2010, the building next door at 113 East Broadway became available and was purchased by Art Reach of Mid Michigan and converted to a gallery and meeting room, with office in the back. Art Reach moved all operations to Art Reach on Broadway in July, 2010, with a grand opening held in mid-August.

The 319 South University location became the home of the Unitarian Universalist Fellowship of Central Michigan church in July, 2010.

330 South University – Important 2010 Change #2. In 1909, G. Jay Stinson came to Mt. Pleasant and opened a funeral home on Broadway Street, later moving into a building on South Normal Street.
Stinson operated the funeral home there for several years with his sons under the name Stinson and Sons Funeral Home, before building a new funeral home in 1940 at 330 South Normal Street, which was renamed College Street, and eventually University Avenue. The building was dedicated in early 1941, and has been in continuous use as a funeral home since then. In addition to   operating the funeral home, an ambulance service was also operated from this same building. Stinson Funeral Home was the last funeral home in the county to have an ambulance service, when it was discontinued in 1963.
Stinson passed away in 1952, and his son, Russell continued to operate the funeral home until his retirement in 1973, when long time employee Harry Helms and his wife Alice purchased the funeral home.
 Helms started working at the funeral home in the early 1940's, working part time while attending Central Michigan College. He served his country during World War II, and came back to Mt. Pleasant and returned to work at the Stinson Funeral Home. After attending mortuary school at Wayne State University, he returned again to work at the funeral home. He passed away in 1980, and his wife, Alice continued operation of the funeral home until her retirement in 2010, when she sold the funeral home to long time employee, Sherman Rowley and his wife Shirley. Sherm has been with the funeral home since November 1979. The name was changed to Rowley Funeral Home in August, 2010.

The January 10, 1994, meeting of the Mt. Pleasant Women's Club celebrated the 100th anniversary of the club's first meeting with a "Hat's Off" theme. Members and guests were asked to wear a hat representing a style popular sometime in the 1894-1994 period. Prizewinners, left to right, were Phyllis Jeppersen (most beautiful hat), Donna Collins (most original), Marianne Richtmeyer (oldest hat), Joyce Prigeon (next oldest hat), Elaine Harris (newest hat), Kathryn Meister (best authentic hat), George Ann Wolf (funniest hat) and Dorothy Adams (best reproduction). The Mt. Pleasant Women's Club was founded by twenty-one women in 1894 as a study club, branching out to many areas of community service over the years with projects including establishing the community's library and raising funds for emergency equipment.

213 South Main Street was the 1951 site of the Grand Opening of Bourland's Television and Appliance Store. Above, James and Bessie Bourland look on while Mayor Del Conkright cuts the ribbon to formally open the store, while appliance representative Ray Brower mades sure the cameraman "got the shot".

The Pere Marquette Hunting and Fishing Club is one of Michigan's oldest such organizations in Michigan. In the 1935 scene above, members and guests gathered the opening day of trout seasoin in front of the clubhouse along the Middle Branch of the Pere Marquette River were, in no particular order: W. Sommerville, F. Warner, C. Riches, E. Bixby, E. Collins, J. Ryan, W. McCall, B. Shangle, Dr. Richardson, Jack Cripo, W. F. Lewis, Walter Russell, W. Schnitzler, E. Palmer, D. Johnson, S. Kelly, Dr. Northway, E. Weidman and Bill Cline. The dogs were not identified by name.

No history of Mt. Pleasant would be complete without mentioning Bernard L. "Buster" Smith, born to drugstore owner Charles and Mamie Smith of Mt. Pleasant in 1919. A Navy veteran, Buster was a ham radio operator (card left), constable, self-appointed Mt. Pleasant Goodwill Ambassador, and photographer. Smith appeared in parades and other Mt. Pleasant and CMU festivities for decades in his constable's uniform until ill health forced his entry into the Grand Rapids Home for Veterans, where he died July 16, 1995.

CHAPTER 15: OIL CAPITAL
Mt. Pleasant Field Proves the whole state is "Oil Hunting Country"

The *Mt. Pleasant Times* of February 27, 1928 reported the discovery of oil in the Pure Root #1 well under a headline reading "CLAIM BEST OIL STRIKE IN THE STATE". The story said that "the drill bit broke through into the oil sand at 3,554 feet", and reported that the strike involved "50 to 60 feet of oil sand." The story said that Pure at the time had about 80,000 acres under lease in the vicinity of the well and others had leased 25,000 acres. In point of fact the strike was the richest of the decade and the fourth largest in the history of the Michigan oilpatch. Eventually 29 million barrels of oil would be pumped from the ground.

For the next several weeks Pure went about the task of getting the well ready for production, while continuing to drill in the area. The company built their own drilling-housing-office complex just south of M-20 so workers would not have to deal with weather and dirt roads to get to the fields that grew up on the company's vast Central Michigan lease holding. Retail operations to serve those workers began nearby and led to establishment of the town of Oil City in Midland County. The name still appears today on Michigan highway maps long after the complex that started the settlement has gone.

The Mt. Pleasant newspaper noted May 29, 1928 that "Walter Russell and Fred Stilgenbauer helped Pure obtain pipeline right of way to Mt. Pleasant." Pure built a pipeline to the Mt. Pleasant railhead and on July 3, 1928 the firm started to sell oil to Imperial Refining, Sarnia, Ontario via rail shipment from Mt. Pleasant.

The pipeline from the Mt. Pleasant Field to the railhead at Mt. Pleasant presented an ideal location to build a refinery in the 600 block of West Pickard Street. Roosevelt Refinery opened in 1930, previous page.

According to *Going Places in Michigan With Leonard Gas,* catalogue for the Clarke Historical Library's February through July 2010 exhibit in the library's gallery in the Park Library, Central Michigan University, Mt. Pleasant Campus: "The discovery of oil in Michigan soon led businessmen in this state to enter it. In 1928 mid-Michigan's Mt. Pleasant oil field was opened and began to produce substantial quantities of crude oil. Two subsequent oil discoveries in the area, in Midland County's Porter Township in 1933 and the Crystal Field in Montcalm County in 1935, made it clear that large amounts of crude oil lay underneath mid-Michigan's ground. Several refineries were constructed to process the crude oil."

"J. Walter Leonard was a young man whose father was a Pennsylvania oil man who was active in oil exploration and development across the nation. The sudden death of one of his father's partners in a Michigan project jeopardized the family interests, and J. Walter was asked to come to the state to ensure the success of the endangered investment. When he arrived, Leonard sensed an opportunity. He bought the drilling rigs his father had sent to Michigan and drilled the wells himself. In 1935 one well, drilled by J. Walter Leonard, The Durban #1 in Montcalm County, opened the very successful Crystal Field. At a time when  production in the state amounted to about 37,000 barrels of oil a day, Leonard's Durban #1 discovery well daily produced an astounding daily figure of 3,594 barrels of oil. J. Walter Leonard suddenly had more oil than he could market. He needed a refinery to process it."

"In 1936, J. Walter Leonard formed a publicly held company which purchased a refinery that was being constructed in Alma, Michigan. The refinery Leonard purchased was small and had very limited technical capability. It could process only 2,500 barrels of crude oil a day, and produce gasoline rated from 40 to 50 octane, which as despairingly called "Michigan gas." Competitors could refine gas rated at 75 to 80 octane. In 1937, the Leonard refinery began a series of improvements designed to both increase capacity and create higher quality products."

"In 1955, Leonard expanded dramatically when it obtained control of two other nearby refineries – Alma's Mid-West Refinery and Mt. Pleasant's Roosevelt Refinery. Because each of the three refineries specialized in different products, the merger was quite successful. However, finding sufficient crude to meet the company's expanded refining capacity proved challenging."

"In 1956 Leonard, which had originally relied on crude oil found in Michigan and increasingly on supplies brought in by pipeline from the south, began to purchase Canadian crude oil. Canadian crude had become available because of a newly completed Canadian oil pipeline that had been built to link Canada's western oil reserves to the country's eastern markets. To lower construction costs, the pipeline traveled through Michigan rather than around it and ended Sarnia, Ontario, where existing pipe could carry the crude further east into Canada."

The Mt. Pleasant Leonard Refinery closed in the mid-1970s. Leonard sold to TOTAL, a French business combine, in the early 1980s, who in turn sold to Diamond Shamrock, a Texas Company, who closed the Alma refinery in 1999.

Now back to the beginning. Following the oil strike east of Mt. Pleasant, several local Mt. Pleasant businessmen became directly involved in the oil industry. In addition to Russell and Stilgenbauer, Virgil McClintic, a Mt. Pleasant attorney, was retained by Pure early to check titles and handle other legal matters. McClintic was later directly involved in the discovery of a natural gas field west of Mt. Pleasant and starting Consumers Power Company, later NOMECO, in the natural gas business. Local butcher Dan Johnson quit selling meat to deal in oil leases. Mt. Pleasant became a boomtown where oilmen were very welcome. In 1929, the Mt. Pleasant Rotary Club hosted a welcome banquet with 40 oilmen as their guests.

Mt. Pleasant became a hub of Michigan petroleum activity, first as an accident of geology and later as a convenience of geography. The community lies close to the geographical center of the "mitten", thus located equal distance from anywhere in the Lower Peninsula. Primary oil and gas explorationists, petroleum supply and service companies, geologists (and later geophysicists), drilling contractors all headquartered in Mt. Pleasant.

Mt. Pleasant became known as the "Oil Capital of Michigan." The town flourished with new residents, new housing, new businesses and best of all, new money.

The Michigan Oil And Gas Association

Prior to the founding of the present Michigan Oil And Gas Association, a group of petroleum folk in the Muskegon area formed an organization in 1928 to establish higher crude oil prices. E. J. Bouwsma, a Muskegon Oil Company employee, was the group's president. However, as the boom at Muskegon subsided and the 1928 Mt. Pleasant Field became the industry's focus, the Muskegon-based association faded away.

However the problems that bedeviled Muskegon oil producers, particularly overproduction causing slumping crude oil prices soon became a problem in the Central Michigan Fields. To deal with these problems producers in Central Michigan, along with those from Muskegon and Saginaw met in Mt. Pleasant and formed the Oil and Gas Producers Association in 1931.

This broader, better financed organization was named the Michigan Oil And Gas Association (MOGA). At a November 27, 1933, meeting in Mt. Pleasant, the newly formed MOGA elected Gordon Oil's Howard D. Atha President.

The Michigan Oil And Gas Association moved offices from Mt. Pleasant to Lansing in the last 1930s and has continued as the voice of Michigan's oil and gas exploration industry to the present day.

Mt. Pleasant oil and gas men have also played an important role in MOGA. Of the Michigan Oil And Gas Associations 40 chief elected officers, 14 have been from Mt. Pleasant: Howard Atha 1934-35-36; W. P. Clarke, 1947; I. W. "Bucky" Hartman, 1951; J. Walter Leonard, 1955-56; E. Allan Morrow, 1957–58; John V. Wicklund, Jr., 1963-64; O. H. Kristofferson, 1965; William C. Myler, 1968-69; G. R. "Rollie" Denison, 1970-71; K. P. Wood, 1972-73; Vance W. Orr, 1984-85; Jack Harkins, 1990-91; Vance W. Orr, Jr., 1992-93; William C. Myler, Jr., 1998-99; and James R. Stark, 2004-05.

Over time, seven individuals have served as the senior staff person of the Michigan Oil And Gas Association. Of those, the longest serving in the Association's history has been Frank L. Mortl, MOGA President in 2010.

Of Mt. Pleasant's 86 mayors through 2010, eight have been from the oil and gas industry: James Leonard - 1947; I. W. "Bucky" Hartman - 1949; Norman X. Lyon - 1950-1951; G. R. "Rollie" Denison – 1956-1957; K. P. Wood – 1960; J. Dean Eckersley - 1964-1966; and Ray Planteroth – 1967-1968.

The official opening ceremonies of the August 11-16, 1935, Michigan Oil and Gas Exposition, above, were conducted by: Joseph P Carey - Central Michigan College/ Mt. Pleasant Planning Commission Chair; William Cline - Lupher Oil; Harry Hunt - Michigan Oil & Gas Association Executive Secretary; P J Hoffmaster - Michigan Conservation Department Director; Howard Atha - Gordon Oil/Michigan Oil And Gas Association President; Roy Taylor; Taylor Brothers Oil Company/Michigan Oil & Gas Exposition Committee Chairman; and Harry Gover - Mt Pleasant Chamber of Commerce President. The Exposition drew more than 25.000 people to Island Park.

The 1935 Michigan Oil and Gas Exposition Opening Parade was led by a hearse bearing an effigy of "Ole Man Depression", which was dumped in the Chippewa River, symbolizing the presence of the oil industry's having spared the town from the financial devastation felt elsewhere. By 1939, the winds of World War II were stirring breezes and the Expositions were suspended, never to be revived again.

So great were the crowds at the Oil & Gas Exposition that overnight a pedestrian bridge was fabricated at bottom of the hill, at the Main Street entrance to the park to avoid vehicle-people mishaps. Note the welder working into the first night of the expo to complete the bridge, left, which was in use well into the 1970s as a pedestrian overpass and "kids on bikes thrill ride".

Road conditions were miserable in the 1920s, so as Pure developed the Mt. Pleasant Field and others in the area, the company built a housing complex for its employees for their easy access to the wells they were drilling, usually in 12 hour shifts, to avoid the dangers of traffic to and from Mt. Pleasant. The stores, and a hotel, that came into being to serve the needs of Pure camp residents is known as Oil City.

The Annual MOGA Picnic/Reunion

Semi-annual banquet gathering for MOGA directors began in the summer of 1934 at Mt. Pleasant.

MOGA Picnic Co-chairmen Muskegon Development's Bill Myler,below left,

and Co-chairman Lease Management's Jack Harkins right, with MOGA President Frank L. Mortl, have greeted annual Picnic/Reunion Michigan and national oilpatch newcomers and veterans since 1978.

From 1934 to 1938, the semi-annual banquets were held. at Mt. Pleasant. In 1939, the first official MOGA Summer Picnic opened to the general membership took place at the Alma home of then MOGA President Harold Mc Clure Sr.. The 1941-1945 World War II years saw limited summer outings (none in 1943 and 1945) in various parts of the state.

In 1946 until the present, the MOGA Annual Picnic/Reunion has been held at the Mt. Pleasant Country Club, shown below in the early 1980s.

The Michigan Oil & Gas News

With projects proposed and underway throughout the Michigan "oilpatch," oilfolk needed a way to keep up with the action. Local newspaper filled some of the information gap but local papers were, by their nature, not interested in the broader, statewide story. Moreover local reporters lacked real knowledge of the industry to help filter true happenings from the promoter's hype.

John Murphy, Jim Dunnigan, Lou Aaronson and Danny Miller, with the backing of financial associates, published the first issue of the *Michigan Oil & Gas News* on June 20, 1933. Besides a number of field stories, the front page of that first issue (in a broadsheet newspaper format) carried a message from the owners saying "We want to give you a service that you need; in return we expect but moderate compensation and your enthusiastic support. An honest living and the feeling we have served, and well, are all the rewards we seek,"

The Michigan Oil & Gas News booth at the 1935 Michigan Oil and Gas Exposition

Dunnigan, Aaronson, and Miller had been college buddies at what is today Detroit's Wayne State University. Miller's father encouraged them to start an oil reporting paper. Murphy was a Mt. Pleasant local whose early thoughts and training were about a career teaching or in the priesthood. Lindy Davis joined the publication in the mid-1930s, as did Norman X. Lyon in 1937. Lyon and Davis both came from the local Mt. Pleasant newspaper.

Davis later went to work for the *Grand Rapids Press*. Lyon took the job to "fill in for awhile." "Awhile" turned out to be a very long time.

From 1937 until 1972, Lyon would alternately be Editor of the *Oil News* and the *Mt. Pleasant Daily Times News*, the local newspaper. After retirement, he continued as a contributor to the Oil & Gas News until his 1991 death.

MOGA was not especially interested in the publication business but it was interested in keeping alive the weekly communications "glue" the magazine provided. MOGA bought the publication rights to the *Oil & Gas News* in December, 1972. For a few

Norman X. Lyon as a Michigan Oil & Gas News correspondent from his Florida winter headquarters in 1982.

months the publication ceased printing, but in March 1973, Jack R. Westbrook, this book's author, was hired as manager and editor. The paper resumed publication in April with Norm Lyon as a consultant..

Dick Bolton, fresh from CMU following U.S. Air Force service, was hired in June of that year to assist Westbrook and edited the publication until 1981 when Bolton left. In 2010, Bolton works for the Mt. Pleasant *Morning Sun* as a photographer and columnist. Ironically, in 1982 Scott Bellinger, present *MOGN* Editor, left the *Morning Sun* to join the *Oil & Gas News*. In 2002, Westbrook retired to become a part-time "contributing editor" and Bellinger replaced Westbrook as managing

214 North Franklin was the home of the Michigan Oil & Gas News weekly magazine from 1933 until 1973. Above, the address is now home to the Green Tree Cooperative Grocery.

editor of the publication. in 2010 with Matt Hewitt, Associate Editor along with Shannon Sak Office Manager.

Walter W. Russell

Walter W. Russell was a native Mt. Pleasantite, born October 9, 1886, He served as mayor of the city in 1917 and was on the City Charter Commission in 1923 and later on the City Commission. He also served on the Mackinac Island Commission. With Charles Carnahan, he was one of the founders of Mt. Pleasant's General Agency, insurance and real estate.

Like Isaac A. Fancher and Samuel W. Hopkins, profiled elsewhere in this book, Walter W. Russell left a monumental but little recognized contribution to the future and prosperity of Mt. Pleasant by almost single-handedly putting Mt. Pleasant on the path to becoming "The Oil Capital of Michigan."

It is not often recognized that the Laura Root #1, discovery of the Mt. Pleasant oil field, was almost astraddle the Isabella/Midland county line. Being located almost equal distance from Mt. Pleasant and Midland, either could have become the place to live, commute to the field, but for Walt Russell's quick thinking and fast action.

When the Mt. Pleasant field discovery well was reportedly looking good in mid 1928, Walter Russell sprung into action, spearheading a group of Mt. Pleasant businessmen who pratically overnight leased pipeline right-of-way from the discovery well to the railhead at Mt. Pleasant, securing an easy route to market for the crude oil from that field, when the discovery well came in August 29, 1928.

The oil, the equipment suppliers, the people and the resultant cashflow, went to Mt. Pleasant instead of Midland, just ahead of the Great Depression. Thanks to Walt and the oil industry, Mt. Pleasant felt little of the Depression's financial chaos.

So if Mt. Pleasant is the Oil Capital of Michigan, Walter W. R. Russell is forever it's godfather.

Though later years have seen the intensity of field activity shift elsewhere in the state, Mt. Pleasant remains a viable center of petroleum industry activity with 97 business entities with Mt. Pleasant addresses listed as doing business with the industry in whole or in part in the 2010 edition of the Michigan Petroleum Directory.

In 2010, Mt. Pleasant is back in the oil and gas exploration and production headlines with a new series of successful wells having been drilled in the past year. New oil discoveries are good news for everybody, mineral owners, tax men, merchants and oilmen, who may feel delighted but maybe not as enthusiastically as Mt. Pleasant independent oilman D.F. Jones, right.

Walter Russell's son-in-law, K. P. Wood was MOGA President 1973-1974 and Russell's grandson, Walter Wood continues in the oil business in Mt. Pleasant.

CHAPTER: 16: WAR MEMORIALS AND PARKS

The Civil War Memorial in Riverside Cemetery in the 800 block of West Broadway is Mt. Pleasant's oldest, erected at an unknown date by the Wa – Bu – No Post 250 of the Grand Army of the Republic. One of 8,600 community posts operating from 1879 until 1948.

World War I Monument – On November 2, 1942, the World War I memorial was unveiled on the median of 100 North Kinney Boulevard by the American Legion and the American Legion Auxiliary. "In Memory of the World War Veterans of Isabella County", the War was not numbered or named, perhaps in the hope there would not be another.

World War II Monument – In 1948, the World War II monument was erected on the opposite side of Broadway on the median at 100 North Kinney Boulevard, reading "Dedicated in loving memory to those brave sons and daughters of Isabella County who served their country in World War II.

On May 24, 1946, the Isabella County Times-News at Mt. Pleasant ran the following Isabella Honor Roll of World War II, presented here in the order they were listed: Dalton Bryce, Leroy Beck, John Burns, Harold E. Brown, Dewey Bundy, John Beltnick, Leo Brown, Robert Clark, Wilbur Callison, Harold Cooley, Russell Curtiss, Quentin Cook, Philip Crowley, Edward Craven, John Conway, James A. Cole, Harold Coldwell, Maurice Chapman, Charles Conroy, Wallace Cornell, Albert DeLong, Charles Dickinson, John S. Epple, Ronald Esch, Clark Eldred, Floyd Fraley, Richard Fall, Raymond Fuller, Joseph Graverette, Chester Gorham, Alex Hoffman, Paul Hellinger, Paul Hensley, Richard Hammond, Harvey Hibbard, Merle Howe, Donie Jones, Benjamin Knipe, Sid Lennox, Gerald McDonald, Stewart McArthur, Milford Morey, Arthur Myers, Phil McGill, Nelson Mahon, Harvey Mead, Max Morey, Clarence Neal, Paul Onstott, Ralph Pankhurst, Frank L. Porter, Edison Pelcher, Alfred Roberts, Dean Rauch, Gerald Stewart, Arthur Skeats, Russell Sharp, Bennie Smith, Cecil Stevens, Frederick Snider, Roy Straight, Donald Swan, John Stefanich, William Tarr, Joe Ulsh, Steve Varga, Malcolm Wardrop Jr., Vernon Welter, Elton Wood, Clayton Weeks, Cleon Wyman, Bruce Winnie and Joseph Woobury.

Korean War Memorial – In a tree-shaded nook in the heart of downtown Mt. Pleasant at Town Center on the northwest corner of Main and Broadway, the Mt. Pleasant Korean War Memorial is a small island of solace there in the midst of downtown.

The Viet Nam Memorial at the north end of Island Park was dedicated on September 17, 1994, and list all the names of the local fallen in that conflict.

The Operation Iraqi Freedom and Operation Enduring Freedom Memorial was dedicated in 2005 at the north end of Island Park near the Viet Nam Memorial commemorates Justin M. Ellsworth USMC and SFC Gregory A. Rodriquez and all who have served in those two operations. "Never Forget Those Who Have Paid the Ultimate Sacrifice" reads the inscription beneath the rifle and helmet standing between a pair of combat boots.

A 1940s Memorial Day Parade marching west on Broadway near the corner of Court and Broadway streets between war memorials typifies the honor Mt. Pleasant pays then and now to those who served in the United States Armed forces, each represented at the front of the parade with Old Glory.

Josephine M. Hartung: July 31, 1915 – May 26, 2010

Nobody represents the indomitable spirit of patriotism, and even feminism before it was called that, better than a softspoken lady with an iron will we knew better as "Jo" Hartung, above, in the 2000 Memorial Day Parade.

Jo was born Josephine Kwiatkowski in Grand Rapids and left the family farm to go to Grand Haven High School back when going to high school was a real effort beyond the educational limitations of rural one-room first to eighth grade curricula. Tough for a male, even tougher for a female in those days when earning an education was viewed as an honorable accomplishment rather than a chore. For high school, Jo proceeded to St. Mary's Nursing School in Grand Rapids, then worked for a time at the University of Michigan Hospital as a Registered Nurse. Then came World War II and Jo answered the call of her country by joining the U.S. Army. She was involved in the Pacific Theater and stationed in Guam and Saipan. After returning home to Grand Rapids and

marrying Howard Hartung, Jo and her new husband moved to Mt. Pleasant where she began working as a nurse at the Mt. Pleasant Home and Training School, later to morph through half a dozen names to become the Mt. Pleasant Regional Center by the time she retired at the top of Administration. She was a member of the Veterans of Foreign Wars Post 3033 and her name appears on a wall honoring women in the Army Nurse Corps at the women's service memorial in Washington DC. Those who worked for and with her throughout her career knew her as a kind lady with a steel fist in the velvet glove. She loved reading, birdwatching, and her country, which is diminished a bit by her passing.

Dick Barz: Central Michigan Area Toys for Tots Founder

The U. S. Marine Corps Reserve Toys for Tots began in 1947 in Los Angeles, California, when Major Bill Hendricks, USMCR, noticed that there was no charity specifically organized to distribute toys to deserving children during the traditional Chriristmas season. Hendricks gathered and distributed over 5,000 toys that year, beginning a program that became an annual nationwide effort, coordinated by the U. S. Marines. Forty-one years later, in 1988, SSgt, Richard A. "Dick" Barz, having lost his wife of 14 years and feeling withdrawn and distraught, attended a meeting for the survivors of the Chosin Reservoir battle of the Korean War, called "the Chosin Few", in Rankin, Michigan. There he heard about the Toys for Tots program for the first time and was inspired to action. With the help of his family, began collecting toys for distribution the first year from his business, Barz North American Van Lines, collecting, sorting, wrapping and distributing about 50 toys in Isabella County that year.

Toys for Tots became an annual family activity. Dick was coordinator as the program expanded to include Clare County. Eventually the Central

Michigan Area Toys for Tots program. Area law enforcement, businesses and a growing pool of volunteers rallied to the cause. By 2006, Dick Barz, dressed in his Marine uniform, left, along with more than 100 volunteers, was able to distribute more than 8,000 toys to 2,400 area kids.

In modern times, toys can no longer be delivered and wrapped because of the volume of donations. Instead there is now a "Toy Distribution Day", when any parent can come and get toys for children otherwise without means for Christmas toys. Coordinators have Santa visit the children, play holiday music, give away popcorn, computer register recipients, sort and distribute toys.

Barz, whose feet and leg problems stem from his being frozen during the Chosin Reservoir campaign of the Korean War, yielded Toys for Tots coordination to his daughter Lucinda (Barz) Clark and retired from active participation in 2008.

Barz has expressed the belief that his life was spared at the Chosin Reservoir so he could begin the program to make Christmas merrier for local kids.

Grand Army of the Republic Wa-Bu-No Post 250 Fort Sheridan Annual Muster at Island Park – This chapter is entitled War Memorials and Parks and here we get the opportunity to pay tribute to both, above, in a 1913 picture of the family of John Neebes. John fought for the Union Army with a Chicago 72nd Wolverine Infantry in the Civil War before taking up farming with his pension in Isabella County's Chippewa Township. He was widowed and at 50 years old married Flora Moore, 20 years old, of Mt. Pleasant. This is his second family.

Each year the Wa-Bu-No Post 250 of the Grand Army of the Republic would hold a one week muster at Mt. Pleasant's new Island Park, furnishing a straw for the tick (sleeping mats), land for a tent, and flour for cooking. Participants furnished their own bed, table and chairs, and stove for cooking.

Left to right above at the August 19-24, 1913, Fort Sheridan Muster are: Grandmother Mary Morse; a cousin Moore took to raise Corabell Morse; Mary, Claribel and Florence Neebes, John Neebes and Frances Neebes, seated is Flora Neebes with the baby Ruth Neebes. John died in 1928, having raised the five girls of his second family.

Right, the same family at the same event in 1919, with Grandma Morse in her formal black hat.

Island Park - The Lincoln Street Bridge off North Main Street extended Lincoln Street westward past Chatterton's Mill across the Pere Marquette railroad tracks to Fancher's Flats (now Island Park), above. In 1909, the land was bought from Isaac Fancher, a canal was dug on the west side of Fancher Flats and the area was renamed Island Park This bridge was replaced in 1915 by a cement arch bridge.

Island Park, 333 North Main - Before the business expansion of Mission Street and residential growth of other areas of town decentralized Mt. Pleasant lifestyles, 35 acre Island Park was the year-round center of sports, recreational and social life. In 2010, Island Park remains Mt. Pleasant's premier destination park The Mt. Pleasant Municipal Swimming Pool was built about 1938 in the southeast segment of Island Park, offering rooftop swimming, locker rooms and showers. Girls made a left circuit of the ground floor while boys made a right, to wade a shallow foot-cleansing pool and climb the steps to the pool.

Island Park (continued) - Wintertime meant the flooding of the ball diamond in front of the Island Park Grandstand for months of fun at the City Ice Rink, with hot chocolate and warm friendships available day and night.

Viewed from Broadway Street looking north, the flooded swimming pool, tennis courts and utility building representing all that remained of the razed grandstand are shown equally awash.

The past few pages have dealt with those things that have been removed from Island Park over the years. In all fairness, we will spend these last Island Park pages talking about what has been added to the park. Above, the area where the farm animal exhibit buildings once stood now boasts a large pavillion, volleyball courts, a fishing platform, continuation for the motorless trail from Pickens Field to Chipp-A-Water Park, a canoe/kayak launch, a footbridge to Nelson Park, the Viet Nam Memorial and, above, the Timber Town playscape, built in the 1980s and maintained by volunteers. Elsewhere in the park, the old Merchant's Building was replaced by a huge community pavilion where the seasonal Farmers Market is held each summer Thursday. The grandstand is replaced by an outstanding network of ball diamonds. The footbridge to Broadway at Oak Street has been refurbished, and a new shuffleboard arena is located in the southwest quadrant of the park.

The area once occupied by the Municipal Swimming Pool in the southeast quandrant of Isalnd Park is now the location of the Mt. Pleasant skate park. Below, the new splash park at Island Park.

Nelson Park, 714 West Broadway – In the above view from the east bank of the Chippewa River near the wooden West Broadway Bridge about 1906, the curve in the Chippewa River north of the bridge is clearly defined and the west bank shows a horse-drawn carriage with occupants looking at the camera from Nelson Park. The road to the left is the road to Riverside Cemetery. The five acre Nelson Park is Mt. Pleasant's oldest park, purchased from Douglas Nelson in 1891. For a time that included the 1930s, the Park was a tourist camping park, and a temporary tent city for families displaced by the Great Depression.. Below, the same scene in 2010, shows the same part of the river, now with a sediment-built island in the center, probably caused by the slowing of the river flow when the millpond dam was removed in 1972. A portion of Mt. Pleasant's Riverside trail is visible replacing the cemetery road since the cemetery is now accessed directly off the 800 block of West Broadway.

Nelson Park (continued) – The Nelson Park Community Zoo, above,. was started in 1964, boasting a variety of Michigan-indigenous animals including a herd of whitetail deer, a raccoon family and a black bear nicknamed Yogi. Generations of young families delighted in watching the awe on the faces of their toddlers coming nose to nose with real live Michigan wildlife in a controlled setting. Over the years, budget considerations and the stridence of overzealous animal right protesters saw the park removed. The bear died and a stealthy overnight operation saw the deer removed in 2006 with an announcement made after the fact, to the joy of a few and the chagrin of folks who actually used the park. In 2001, a fishing platform was added at the east edge of the park, near the island mentioned on the previous page. Isabella Bank and Trust donated the Centennial Gardens in honor of their 100th Anniversary in 2002, with a bronze Yogi eternally trying to snag a bronze trout with his paw, where once stood the original live bear's home.

Chipp-A-Waters Park, 1403 West High Street – Established in 1963, 30 acre Chipp-A-Waters Park began with a simple canoe/kayak landing with picnic tables. In 2010, the park has playground equipment, an open-air shelter and modern restrooms. June 25, 2010 saw the Access Adventure addition to the park, offering a wheelchair accessible bridge linking upland and wetland trails to the park. At the same time the Mt. Pleasant River Trails system was renamed the GLB River Trail in honor of the late Greg L. Baderschneider, Mt. Pleasant Parks and Recreation Department Director.

Horizon Park , 1535 Sweeney Street – The Mt. Pleasant Schools/City of Mt. Pleasant 22.5 acre East Side Development became Horizon Park in 2000 with a $155,000 grant from the Chippewa Indian Tribe. Through 2004 improvements were made with the grant and in 2010 the park has three soccer fields, a softball field, a tennis court, football field, and quarter-mile paved fitness trail at the corner of Preston and Sweeney streets.

Millpond Park, 607 South Adams to 500 East Broadway – The key element to this 90 acre park is the old millpond dam area originally constructed as a holding area and sluice for logs in 1866 by Harper Brothers to supply power to their saw mill and later the mill race supplied power to Harris Milling Company. A spectacular millpond occupied many, many acres, used for recreational purposes by the citizens of Mt. Pleasant. A boathouse once occupied the east shore of the millpond, as did the ice house built by William T. Tice in 1901. By 1910, Tice was harvesting 1,700 tons of ice per year from the pond, stored and used in iceboxes all over town year-round. In 1955, Floyd Axtell was going to fill in land alongside Adams Street at the west edge of the millpond land for a planned shopping mall, dredging logs and fill dirting a strip in the 700 block of South Adams. The mall never happened but a picnic shelter, playground equipment and, for awhile, a swimming area now sit in the spot. The dam was closed down and the bottomland retrieved as wooded nature areas in 2002, as part of the City's Chippewa River Restoration program, partially financed by an $800,000 grant from the Michigan Natural Resources Trust Fund, a fund derived from

revenues from oil and gas exploration and production on Michigan-owned mineral properties and used to acquire and improve public recreation lands. Five weirs and a three pedestrian bridge trail system were installed, below. The area is a favorite of walkers, kayakers, and bird watchers, just steps from downtown.

Mission Creek Woodland Park, 458 North Harris Street – The land for this 60 acre park along the Mission Creek was acquired and developed in the 1972-1976 period. The park has two open-air shelters, picnic tables with grills, nature trails, playground equipment and, as the kids say "an awesome sledding hill.' Mission Creek was once a major "waterpath" from the western part of the county close to Brady's mission school through the Indian Industrial School land to the Chippewa River.

Sunnyside Park, 1511 Elm Street – 17 acres along Elm Street on Mt. Pleasant's west side just south of West Pickard was improved in 1997 with the installation of soccer fields. The Park in 2010 has a six-field soccer and T-Ball complex, a basketball court, open air Shelter and picnic tables with grills. We didn't mention it specifically but all the city parks are equipped with restrooms .... It goes without saying, so we didn't.

Pickens Field, 309 West High Street – This 15 acre park is just north by the footbridge from Island Park and serves as the northern sourcepoint of Mt. Pleasant's GLB River Trail system. The park has two Little League fields and two Farm League/Softball fields and playground equipment. The site's lowlands have been used on occasion as a staging area for antique cars for the Mt. Pleasant Rods in the Park event.

And as a final word, we want to express our thanks to Bob Banta, left in a pose you'll best recognize him ... with a camera and a smile. Bob, a former radio DJ and retired deputy sheriff, has become a devoted unofficial photographic chronicler of our area and was allowed into the Borden Building during all stages of the renovation. He graciously shared those and many other pictures with the author for this book. We can think of no better way to use this final editorial page of this tome to say:
"Thanks Bob".

Photo Credits

MARY ELLEN BRANDELL
ROBERT BANTA
RICHARD BRANDELL POSTCARD COLLECTION, Clarke Historical
  Library, CMU, Mt. Pleasant Campus;
BILL CAIN
JOE CASCARELLI
CLARKE HISTORICAL LIBRARY, Park Library Building, Central
  Michigan University, Mt. Pleasant Campus
CATHERINE COTTON
JOHN CUMMING
SHIRLEY MARTIN DECKER
PEGGIE EDMONDS
PAUL ELLIOTT
DARLENE FEDEWA
BOB FREI, BEAVERTON mi
FRED GANNON
FRANK GRUSS
GLADYS HALL
JANET HOMAN
MILAN JOHNSON, Overland Park, Kansas;
HUDSON KEENAN
BART LABELLE
NORMAN X. LYON COLLECTION, Clarke Historical Library:
RANDY MARTIN
JOYCE McCLAIN
AGNES MCDONALD
WILLIAM McEWAN photos courtesy SHERRY SPONSELLER
MICHIGAN OIL & GAS NEWS
MI OIL & GAS NEWS COLLECTION, Clarke Historical Library, CMU,
  Mt. Pleasant Campus
MT. PLEASANT (MICHIGAN) AREA HISTORICAL SOCIETY; ALAN
  SHINAVAR photos courtesy SHERRY SPONSELLER;
JACK NEYER
VERN OWENS
JOHN W. PETERS
LYNDA PRIOR, Traverse City MI
PETER REALE
SHIRLEY SHEPPARD
PATRICIA SHOOK
BILL SOWLE
SHERRY SPONSELLER
JOHN STRAIGHT
ROGER WING
VAL WOLTERS
SANDRA HOWARD WOOD

Unless otherwise noted, all of the people credited here are from Mt. Pleasant, MI
Apologies with anyone accidently forgotten.

Bibliography

Portrait and Biographical Album, Isabella County Michigan. Chicago IL; Chapman Brothers, 1884.

Child, Gerald Dwight, Sr., The Campbell Building, Genealogical Society of Isabella County, Mt. Pleasant MI 1999.

Clarke Historical Library, Park Library, *Archives,* Central Michigan University, Mt. Pleasant MI campus.

Cumming, John. *The First 100 Years; A Portrait of Central Michigan University 1892-1992.*Mount Pleasant, MI; Central Michigan University Press, 1992.

Cumming, John. *This Place Mount Pleasant.* Mt. Pleasant, MI; Central Michigan University Press, 1989.

Fancher, Isaac A. *Past and Present of Isabella County Michigan.* Indianapolis IN; B. F. Bowen & Company, 1911.

Isabella County Genealogical Society. *Isabella County, Michigan, Families and History.* Paducah KY; Turner Publishing, 2003.

Johnson, Charles F. *Isabella County.* Grand Rapids; Unpublished manuscript, 1991.

Miller, H. A. and Charles J, Seely. *Faces and Places Familiar.* Mt Pleasant MI Courier Press, 1906.

Numerous websites, newspapers and special events brochures.

Shepherd Historical Society. *Isabella County 1982.* Dallas TX; Taylor Publishing, 1982.

About the Author

JACK R. WESTBROOK is a Mt. Pleasant, Michigan, resident, retired Managing Editor of the Michigan Oil & Gas News magazine and author of five previous historical photo review books for Arcadia Publishing Company: *MICHIGAN OIL & GAS; MT. PLEASANT (Michigan) THEN AND NOW; CENTRAL MICHIGAN UNIVERSITY; ISABELLA COUNTY (Michigan) 1859-2009,* and with co-author historian/genealogist Sherry Sponseller, *YESTERDAY'S SCHOOL KIDS OF ISABELLA COUNTY.*

NOTE: Copies of the photographs contained in this book, in an 8" by 10" glossy format suitable for framing, are available for $10.60 each, including tax and shipping. Please note page number and position on the page when ordering, along with checks made out to ORSB-MtP, P.O. Box 16, Mount. Pleasant MI 48804-0016.

–

Made in the USA
Lexington, KY
31 October 2010